I0828263

IMAGES
of America

AROUND CARTHAGE AND WEST CARTHAGE

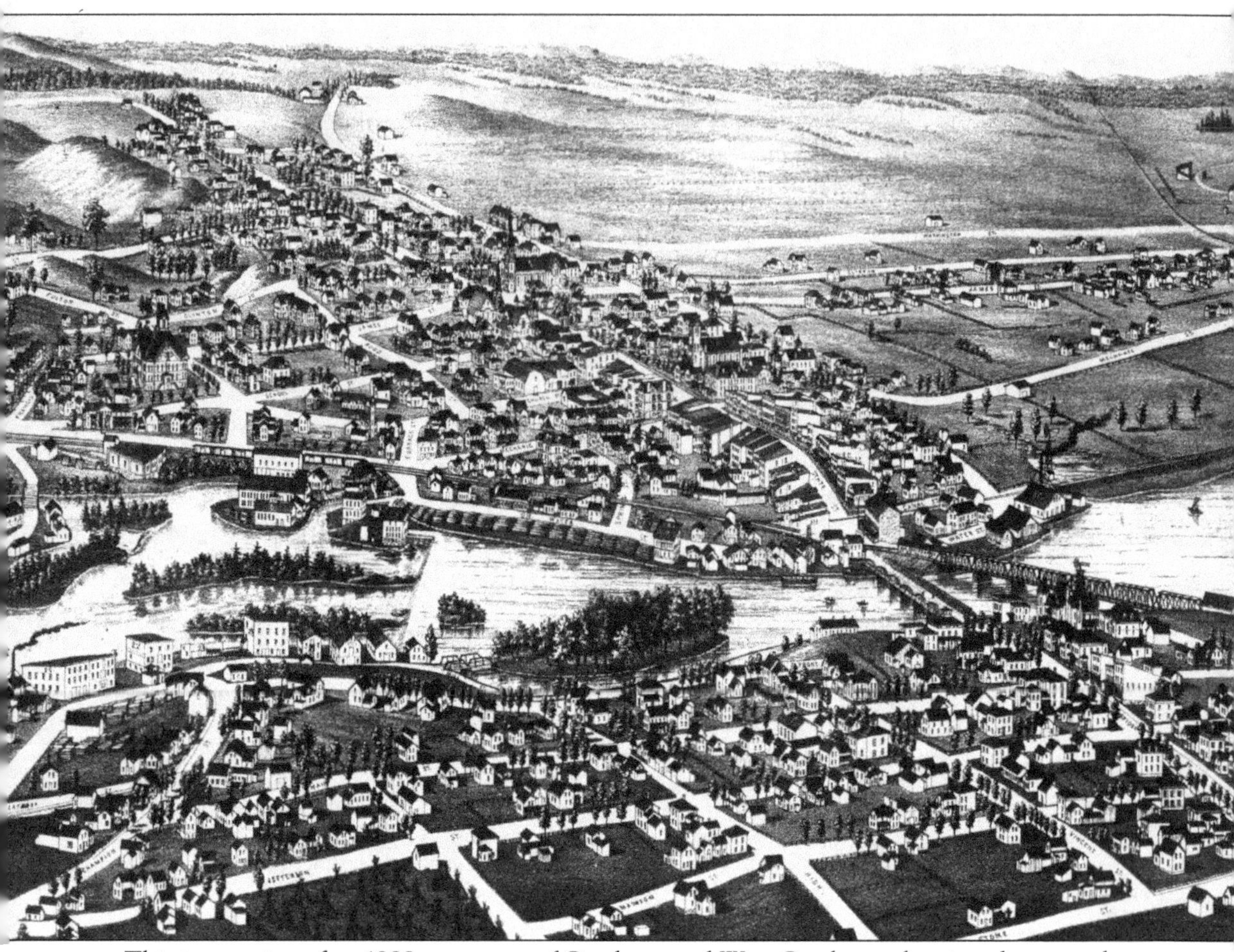

This is a section of an 1888 panorama of Carthage and West Carthage, showing the area where the primary manufacturing of the day was done and much of the residential areas of both villages. When looking at this, it is important to remember that this was drawn just four short years after the great fire of 1884.

On the cover: Please see page 21. (Arnot collection.)

IMAGES
of America

AROUND CARTHAGE AND WEST CARTHAGE

Lynn M. Thornton

ARCADIA
PUBLISHING

ISBN 978-1-5316-3667-8

Published by Arcadia Publishing
Charleston SC, Chicago IL, Portsmouth NH, San Francisco CA

Library of Congress Catalog Card Number: 2007941418

For all general information contact Arcadia Publishing at:
Telephone 843-853-2070
Fax 843-853-0044
E-mail sales@arcadiapublishing.com
For customer service and orders:
Toll-Free 1-888-313-2665

Visit us on the Internet at www.arcadiapublishing.com

To Jack, who made this possible. You have always encouraged me to be all I could be. Thank you.

CONTENTS

Acknowledgments

Carthage and West Carthage are two separate villages inextricably joined by their shared histories. Nothing can show this better than a voyage back to their beginnings. Laura Prievo and the records of the Heritage Room at the Carthage Free Library, Harold Sanderson and the Village of West Carthage archives, Suzanne Wiley and the wealth of materials she amassed during her tenure as Town of Champion historian—all these have proven invaluable in researching this book. Dr. Timothy Abel and Christine Colon of the Jefferson County Historical Society provided information along the way, as have the archives of the *Carthage Republican Tribune* (CRT) and the materials, including insurance maps published by the Sanbourn Map Company, gathered by Sean McHale and others in hopes of establishing a papermaking museum and maintained by Linda Wier. Many thanks to Paul Brown and Laban Haverstock of Metro Paper Industries, who made photographs available; to Gary Wood, historian of the American Legion who opened the legion's books; and to the individuals who generously loaned materials, especially pictures. Among those who made private collections available are Bob Blunden and his son, Bill, Delena Schreck, Henry Watkins, Jeannie Fox, Michael Perfetto Jr., Rita McLean, and Agnes King. Thank you also to Fritz Metzger for invaluable papermaking information; Rebekah Collinsworth, my wonderful editor at Arcadia Publishing, for her help and support throughout this project; and all the people in the community who offered suggestions, stories, and encouragement. Unless otherwise noted, all images are from the author's collection.

Introduction

In the beginning was the river. Flowing north then westward between verdant banks, the Black River has served many generations, providing power, transportation, recreation, and drinking water for thousands of people. Native Americans followed its course into their hunting lands, referring to it as the "Dismal Wilderness," and generally chose to live elsewhere. Early pioneers followed the river north from Lyons Falls and usually left the river before reaching the series of rapids that gave the original settlement the name of Long Falls.

In 1798, Henri Boutin purchased 1,000 acres on the east side of the river from Rudolph Tillier, an agent of the French Company. With a team of men, he began to clear the land but unfortunately was drowned in some manner (accounts vary). Vincent LeRay purchased his land at auction.

At nearly the same time, Jean Baptiste Bossuot of Troyes, France, came to America with Baron Wilhelm von Steuben (who later served with George Washington at Valley Forge) and remained at Long Falls after Boutin's death, maintaining a ferry and an inn for travelers, both on the bank of the Black River. The ferry ran until the first bridge was built in 1812–1813. In later years, his home was on the corner of Dock and Canal Streets, which probably was the site of the inn he ran with the help of his wife. Bossuot died in Champion in 1847 at the age of 93.

When a post office was established about 1814, the name of Long Falls was changed to Carthage. Up to that time post riders had carried the mail. About 1833, LeRay established his land office on West Street in Carthage, which made the community even more important. The original title to all the lands in Carthage has since been derived from LeRay's holdings.

At Carthage, the river expands into a broad and rapid stream spanned by a 500-foot bridge. There is also a railroad bridge a short distance above that crosses the river at a diagonal. Just at the beginning of the falls, a state dam was built in 1855 reaching from shore to shore, a distance, at that point, of 900 feet. The river at Carthage was a perfect place for industries, utilizing the drop of 55 feet in less than a mile for almost unlimited waterpower. As a consequence, during the 19th century and well into the 20th, a number of industries lined the banks on both sides of the river as well as on the many islands that stud this section.

The river watched the rise and demise of sawmills, flour mills and gristmills, sash and blind factories, a veneer mill, foundries and machine shops, the electric light works, and a number of paper mills. Today there are several paper mills and a machine shop; most of the rest are but distant memories. The number of people who made their living in the paper and wood product fields has shrunk dramatically as mills burned, were abandoned, or moved in search of a cheaper workforce.

The State Dam was not the first dam the twin villages saw; in 1806, David Coffeen came to Long Falls and began the erection of a gristmill on the west bank of the river. He also constructed a dam, extending diagonally up the stream from his mill, but not across the channel. The owners of the forge on the east side subsequently completed this dam. LeRay built the forge in 1816, and about the same time, he was largely responsible for the construction of the highway leading from Long Falls to the St. Lawrence River, known as the Alexandria Road. Also under LeRay's direction, Claudius S. Quilliard built a blast furnace in 1819. The old forge burned soon after it was built, but in the following years, a larger capacity furnace was built. These blast furnaces eventually led to the founding of machine shops, which arose to complement the paper industry and other businesses on the riverbanks.

At the same time, as settlers continued to arrive, Carthage continued to grow. In 1812, the legislature authorized the construction of a toll bridge across the river, and in 1812–1813, the structure was built under the direction of Ezra Church. In 1829, because the old bridge was in bad repair, a new free bridge was discussed, and through the work of LeRay, Joseph C. Budd, and others, a set of five free bridges was built, from island to island, across the river. This series of bridges lasted less than two years, floods taking their toll. By this time, the upper bridge had been repaired and made free (1829), and former tollgate keeper Seth Hooker no longer collected fares. In 1840, a new covered bridge was built on the site, and by an act passed on April 11, 1853, the state assumed charge of the structure, rebuilt it, and since has remained in charge of the bridge. The work was completed in 1854, and in the next year, the state also built the substantial dam below the bridge, at the head of the falls. That bridge lasted until 1896. Since that time, there have been several more bridges crossing the Black River at the same point.

These bridges were necessary, for by this time, Carthage had become a hamlet of some note, and many businessmen there preferred to live on the highlands on the west side. Foot traffic was brisk. About 1840, Henry D. Cadwell opened a general store on the west side; as the population increased and as business interests grew in the hamlet, the name of West Carthage was adopted.

At the same time, business thrived on the east side. Three taverns, two groceries, two large and elegant churches, one oil mill, one flax mill, two blast furnaces, warehouses, one stone schoolhouse, one frame schoolhouse, two blacksmith shops, one stone nail factory and rolling mill, one large stone machine shop, one large stone ax factory, one large stone tannery, one large stone flouring mill, three sawmills, three cabinet and chair shops, two land offices, two physicians and apothecary shops, two lawyers' offices, one cupola furnace, two forges, and two carpenter shops were estimated by Leonard G. Peck to exist there by 1839.

Education was an important part of the growth of the twin villages; in the early history of the area, the entire territory was divided into three districts, and provision was made for the maintenance of a school in each. In 1828, the same territory was redistricted, and the hamlet called Long Falls was in district No. 3. About that time, a schoolhouse was built on School Street, near State Street. It was a substantial structure and served for several years. Another school was opened about 1830 by Arby Leonard. This, however, was a private school. Harrison Wilbur succeeded Leonard and in 1842 built an academy on the present Elks Club site at School and Fulton Streets, to which he gave the name Carthage Academy. This was the school that burned in the 1884 fire.

The first schoolhouse in West Carthage was built about 1832 on a plot of land on the corner of Champion and Jefferson Streets, conveyed to the district by A. Champion. At that time, the school building was in the center of the district, which comprised quite a section of the farming land located beyond and toward the hamlet of Champion.

In 1856, the residents of the West Carthage area decided to have a school of their own and accordingly purchased a lot on the corner of Jefferson and Vincent Streets. This was in April 1858, and during that year, the schoolhouse was built. The building was enlarged and remodeled 12 years later. This former school building later became the village hall and fire station, until it was torn down in 1990 when the new municipal complex was built across from P&C Plaza on High Street.

In the school year of 1903–1904, West Carthage School secured the right to have regents examinations. Before that time, anyone wishing to take regents had to go to Carthage High

School. As early as 1900, there was talk of having a new building to accommodate the overflow in the old school. In 1905, it was decided to pay $28,000 for a new building and to sell the old site to the Village of West Carthage for $2,000. That same year, the new building was opened for use, equipped in a very modern fashion with electric lights and other conveniences. Classes were started in the fall of 1905, and the first graduating class to have the honor was the class of June 1906, which consisted of one member, Robert A. Hughes.

In communities where wood played such a major role, fire departments always have been very important. Prior to the incorporation of the Village of Carthage, the apparatus for extinguishing fires was primitive, and the department was composed of the village population, without regular order or recognized head. However, after the corporation act in 1841 was passed, the trustees set about organizing a fire department and on July 24 formed a company, Carthage No. 1, with Samuel A. Budd as captain. On August 12, 1842, a hand engine was purchased, and on June 9, 1843, Washington Fire Company was formed. The large cistern at the corner of State and School Streets was built in 1849. A hook and ladder company was organized on May 24, 1851, with Levi Wood as captain, and on April 9, 1852, and again on December 20, 1870, similar companies were organized. Carthage Hook and Ladder Company, a permanent organization, was formed on June 12, 1874. Hose companies were soon organized, Nos. 1 and 2, of which Tiger and Rescue Hose companies grew from. The steam engine, a No. 2 Silsbee, was purchased as a result of a resolution of the trustees passed in February 1875. Reservoirs were constructed at convenient points in the village and were used until the completion of the waterworks in 1893.

On March 4, 1896, the West Carthage Fire Department was organized with 38 charter members and David Trembly as the first chief. The fire department consisted of two companies, known respectively as the M. P. Mason and W. B. Van Allen Hose Companies. "Each had a good hose cart and sufficient supply of serviceable hose on its reel," according to department records. John Coburn initially offered his barn at 2 Bridge Street for use of the fire department. When Coburn needed his barn, the fire department moved to Eugene Buck's barn at 27 Bridge Street, where it remained until 1905, when the village bought the schoolhouse located at the corner of Jefferson and Vincent Streets and converted it to the village hall. The West Carthage Hook and Ladder Company was organized at some time after 1906, and the name was changed to E. H. Austin Hook and Ladder Company on June 14, 1915. Before the fire department was officially organized, men in the village were on night fire watch every night. The bell of the Congregational church or the "mocking bird" whistle of the sulphite mill alerted those who went to fires.

On June 7, 1892, the qualified electors of Carthage voted to issue bonds to the amount of $50,000 to be used in constructing a water supply system. The work was begun by contractors Moffett, Hodgkins, and Clark of New York City in the fall of 1892 and was completed and accepted on June 1, 1893. The system consisted of a pumping station on Guyot's Island, where water was taken from the river and forced to a standpipe (75 feet high and 20 feet in diameter) erected on an elevation in the eastern part of the village. Carthage was supplied with an abundance of water for all domestic purposes, and an additional means of extinguishing fires was provided. Meanwhile, in West Carthage, a contract for constructing the waterworks had been made, and in January 1896, the system was completed and accepted by the board of commissioners. The water supply was obtained from Carthage, the main pipe being extended across the river and through the village streets. For the water, the local board paid the Carthage commissioners $500 annually.

With the infrastructure in place, the scene was set for the advent of the industry that would forever change the economy of the twin villages, for good or ill. The pulp and paper mills began to flourish up and down the shores of the Black River. James A. Outterson led the way; between 1881 and 1904, he bought and/or managed 15 paper mills in the North Country, including the Carthage Tissue Paper Mills Company (1897); the Carthage Sulphite and Pulp Company (1898); the Champion Paper Company (1901); the West End Paper Company (1901); and the LeRay Paper Company (1904). In 1911, he merged the Carthage Sulphite and Pulp Company and the LeRay Paper Company into the Carthage Sulphite Pulp and Paper Company. By 1923,

Carthage had 20 manufacturing establishments, and by 1924, the annual total production of pulp and paper products for the twin villages was 100,000 tons. The National Paper Products Company, a division of Crown Zellerbach Corporation, came in 1915 and in 1917 bought all the properties of the Carthage Tissue Paper Mills. Gradual expansion followed until the mid-1980s when a number of economic factors began to force mill owners to begin looking elsewhere for materials and workforce.

One name that began in the early 1900s still remains strong in the paper industry of northern New York, that of Hirschey. Urban C. Hirschey helped establish Climax Manufacturing Company. The company, founded by Hirschey's brother Samuel in 1904, initially made incubators then switched to a new form of packaging, the folding box. Urban joined his brother in business in 1910 and upon Samuel's death in 1918 became president of the company. During the years between World War I and World War II, Climax Manufacturing Company was able to take advantage of the explosion in packaging to expand operations and acquire an idle mill in Carthage in 1938, to make its own board and paper products. Carthage Papermakers continues to supply the Lowville plant with these materials.

But as materials began to dry up, most of the mills needed to look farther afield, and the southern pine led many of them to relocate on the coastal plains of the southern United States. Many stretches of the Black River now reflect the dead eyes of shuttered mills.

One

EARLY INDUSTRIES

This is a sketch of the LeRay blast furnace built in 1819 on the site of the present New York Central Railroad depot by James LeRay de Chaumont. Calling it the Carthage Iron Works, LeRay advertised that it was producing potash kettles, stoves (box stoves, oval oven stoves, cookstoves, plate stoves), and pig iron.

CARTHAGE IRON WORKS.

The Furnace has been, and will continue for some time in blast: The Potash Kettles, Stoves and the ware in general, are acknowledged to be at least equal in quality to any made or imported in the state, and are put at very low prices.

The stoves are, box stoves 2 1-2 and 3 feet; oval oven stoves 22, 24, and 28 inches; cooking stoves 2 kinds large size; small seven plate stove; 10 plates stove with oven and boiler, two sizes. The above are from 10 to 35 dollars; cash is required for the oval stoves: the rest of the ware will be sold for approved notes, or for good merchantable wheat, oats or corn, and pork, on delivery of the articles. The Pigs are of a superior quality for Bar Iron, or for castings in general. Pipes will also be sold with the stoves, if desired, for cash.

Also on hand an assortment of Bar Iron of excellent quality.—*January*, 1823.

V. LE RAY DE CHAUMONT.

This is an advertisement by Vincent LeRay de Chaumont for the goods and services of his blast furnace located on Mechanic Street, at the present site of the New York Central Railroad depot. (Heritage Room Collection.)

Gifford Sawmill workmen are shown in this 1900 picture. Some identified men are Tom La Lone (third from left, second row), Joe Miner (third from left, third row), Doc Kendall (fifth from left, third row), Henry King (sixth from left, third row), George Ellinsworth, father-in-law of Bill Hale (ninth from left, third row), Jay Goutremont (tenth from left, third row), Alec La Lone (eleventh from right, third row), Bob Montgomery (front center), and young Henry Champion (extreme right, first row). As seen in the image below, fire destroyed this mill around 1920. (CRT archives.)

This is the Coburn Sawmill about 1885. This mill was the only one to survive the 1884 fire and immediately began 24-hour shifts to cut wood brought to Carthage by lumbermen who doubled their efforts to keep the mill supplied. H. Van Amber of Castorland opened a lumberyard on the dock to assist in the rebuilding. The picture below was taken from Coburn Hill above the mill, showing the State Dam to the left and logs waiting to be taken ashore in the foreground. (Town of Champion Archives.)

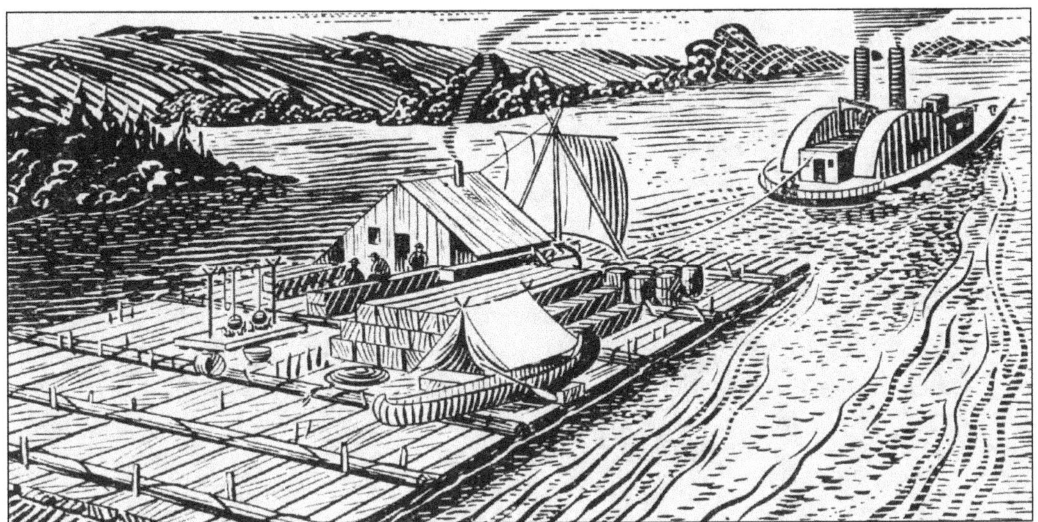

Lumber frequently came to Carthage from mills in Castorland, Beaver Falls, and other points between there and Lyons Falls. Sometimes it was formed into rafts and pulled by tugs. It was often off-loaded at the foot of West Street, where there were docks and warehouses. Charles Brownell recalls helping to tie up such a freight boat as a lad in his book *They Called Me Chuckie*. This sketch is from William D. Welsh, around 1941.

This 1899 picture shows the piles of sawed wood in the yards of the Carthage Lumber Company. This facility was located on Front Street in West Carthage. (Meyer collection.)

Seen here are employees of the Meyer and Farrar Furniture Factory, Champion Street. From left to right, they are (first row) Jim Waite, Pat Noone, and William Farrar; (second row) L. Barthelemew, unidentified, Charles Meyer, Fred Cooley, George Trainer, Charles Baxter, Pierre Meyer, Celon (Ed) Bushnell, William Burt, and Wright Thayer; (third row) John Prievo, Orlando Rice, and John Reed. This photograph was taken about 1900. (Meyer collection, Heritage Room.)

Variously known as the S. Gibbs Doors and Sash Factory and the Vrooman Sash and Blind Factory, this building was located on the west side and was one of several that made the window frames and interior blinds used in homes of the period. (Meyer collection.)

Two

Early Business District

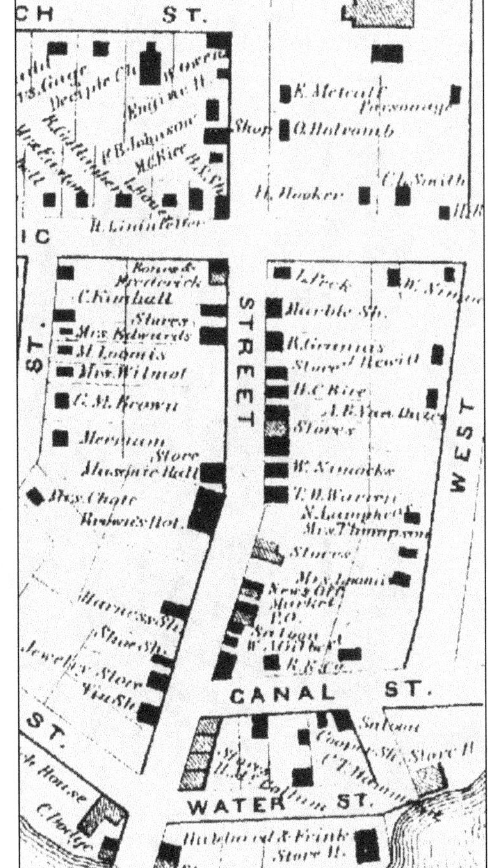

The early 1900s were a booming time for the twin villages. There were all types of merchants and services available to the citizens, numerous churches, hotels, and societies existed, and the business district of Carthage and West Carthage centered on State, Mechanic, and Bridge Streets. Although this map is from 1864, it was clearly a busy time.

The Levis House, shown in 1909, was the original site of the Hatch House (1840–1861). After burning, it was rebuilt in 1862 by Remsen Brown then sold in 1870 to Orville Levis. Federal agents raided it in 1925, and a quantity of near beer was confiscated. After a long history of serving the public, it was finally sold at auction in 1992 and torn down in 2002.

Brownell Print Shop at 30 South Mechanic Street in 1899 had the motto "Prints everything that is printable." (Heritage Room Collection.)

Dr. Frank Lord, dentist, had his office on the second floor of the Strickland Building. Later years saw other dentists in the same office; Dr. Walter Day and Dr. Bernard McDermott had the office above the clock, on the front corner.

Meyers Furniture Store is seen here, with local young people in front. Note the rifle in front of the young woman on the right. This is one of a series of photographs taken by Pierre Meyer of West Carthage between 1890 and 1910. (Heritage Room Collection.)

The Eggleston Block, across from St. James' Roman Catholic Church, later the home of the *Carthage Republican Tribune*, was damaged but not destroyed by the great fire of 1884. When the building was demolished for the current Kinney Drugs, some artifacts were found that might have related to the fire. (Heritage Room Collection.)

The Grand Union Hotel, formerly the Carthage Inn, is now the site of the addition to the Carthage Savings and Loan on State Street. Michael Gleason built it in 1893. Frank Pinnizzotto added the brick facade in 1935. (Heritage Room Collection.)

The Hubbard Block contained Mendelsohn's Gentleman's Clothing Store as well as Porter and Porter Law Offices on the second floor. G. W. Schmid had a jewelry, clock, and silverware shop. In the *c.* 1900 image below, Issac Mendelsohn is on the right, and William Arnot is next to him. Note the wooden sidewalk. Mendelsohn, born in Kovno, Russia, came to America in 1885 and began his career in northern New York as a peddler with a backpack. After two years, he employed a cart and horse and after seven years (1895) opened his first Carthage store. He was located in the Hubbard Block for 31 years and the next 8 in the Schmidt Block. He died in 1952 at the age of 90. (Arnot collection.)

This photograph of the business district taken in 1900 clearly shows the National Exchange Bank on the corner of North Mechanic and State Streets. Immediately to the right are the Surprise Store (later Noland's) and the Carthage Cigar and Pool Room. The next building is the Grand Union Hotel (just the edge of the porch is visible).

Kesler Shoes (on the corner of State and North Mechanic Streets) eventually became Faye Kamide's Boot Shop, where generations of Carthaginians purchased their shoes and boots. This building, at the time Clemons Plumbing and Heating, was lost in a 2002 fire. (Bob Blunden collection.)

Villar's Drug Store, later a Rexall store then Fox Drugs, was finally lost to fire in 2002 and is now part of the new community green space. The facade underwent major changes along the way. (Suzanne Wiley collection.)

The Dunlap Block, currently the home of the Carthage Book Store, was home to many businesses over the years, including Carthage Electric Light and Power Company and, during the mid-1900s, Sherman Electric. (Bob Blunden collection.)

Located in the center of town, the Elmhirst was located where HSBC is now found. It was directly across the street from the National Exchange Bank and only a block from the New York Central Railroad depot. Traveling salesmen frequently made overnight stops, as did visitors to the community. (Bob Blunden collection.)

Pictured is Garthe and Company at 93 State Street. It is listed in the 1904 Carthage business directory as a pork packer, the "Most up To-Date Market in Northern New York." It further says that Otto Garthe was a dealer in fresh- and saltwater fish, oysters, vegetables, eggs, canned goods, and soap. (Heritage Room Collection.)

The Springsteen Store, in this 1899 picture, is the current site of the Velaro gas station on the corner of Bridge and North Main Streets. (Bob Blunden collection.)

This next picture is about 10 years later, showing the addition of the Balmat and Brayton Hardware and Plumbing Store. The building later became the Accarino Brothers grocery store and meat market, seen below in the 1940s. There were meat lockers in the building on the left that individuals could rent. (Below, Town of Champion Archives.)

The image above is looking up State Street toward the National Exchange Bank (currently known as the Buckley Building). There are a few automobiles, but mostly horse-drawn vehicles still travel the dirt streets. The globed lighting shown here are gaslights, probably lit at dusk by Fred Klingner, the village lamplighter. Electric lights were first turned on in 1887. Carthage was one of the first towns to become "illuminated" in this part of the state. The picture below, from the 1899 Carthage and West Carthage directory, shows the initial telephone poles and an early fire hydrant, but it must predate the one above due to the absence of gaslights. (Above, Bob Blunden collection.)

The McCollum Block, erected in 1833, is shown in lower right of photograph above. Clark Dodge, for many years a prominent merchant on State Street, built the Dodge Block (seen below), which burned in 1861, and a fine residence on State Street, which burned in the fire of 1884. In his early life, he was a wagon maker, and he ended his life as a banker in Boonville. One can make out a rocking chair on the roof of the building near the center of town, signifying the presence of a furniture store. (Town of Champion Archives.)

Scander Maroun was one of the first of a number of Lebanese businessmen who settled in Carthage. A native of Bekahotoota, Lebanon, he arrived in 1900, working first with his brother Abdoo for four years before founding his own grocery and clothing store at 211 State Street. Abdoo operated a dry goods store right across the railroad tracks from his brother at 221 State Street. Both brothers remained a vital part of the business district until their deaths. (Town of Wilna Archives.)

Michael Gleason built the Grand Union Hotel in 1893. In 1905, owners Melvin and Laura Quinn were arraigned for selling liquor on Sunday. They pleaded not guilty to the charges and bail was fixed $500 apiece. Those were the times where cards, liquor (at the wrong time), and women of questionable repute were grounds for raiding an establishment. (Town of Champion Archives.)

This is probably Fred Marquette's bar on lower State Street, next to the railroad tracks, around 1900. (Town of Champion Archives.)

Beyers Drug and Merchandise Store, on the corner of Bridge and South Main Streets, is shown here about 1900. This was the location of the House of Dobson for many years, as well as the Cabbage Rose, a computer store. It is now the Amy Earle School of Dance. (Michael Perfetto Jr. collection.)

About 1900, this cavalry parade passes up State Street toward the military reservation of Pine Camp (possibly called Camp Hughes at that time). The McCollum building is in the left background. (Town of Champion Archives.)

The picture above shows State Street before paving. Early fire reports mention equipment becoming mired down in the mud, especially on lower State Street, which was heavily traveled. In some photographs, there are wooden crosswalks in evidence; there may be one at the corner of State and Mechanic Streets in the center of this picture, as well as the one in front of the Levis House. In the image below, men start laying brick pavement on State Street. In the background (right) are the Windsor and the Irvington Hotels. (Town of Wilna Archives.)

Three

Islands and Bridges

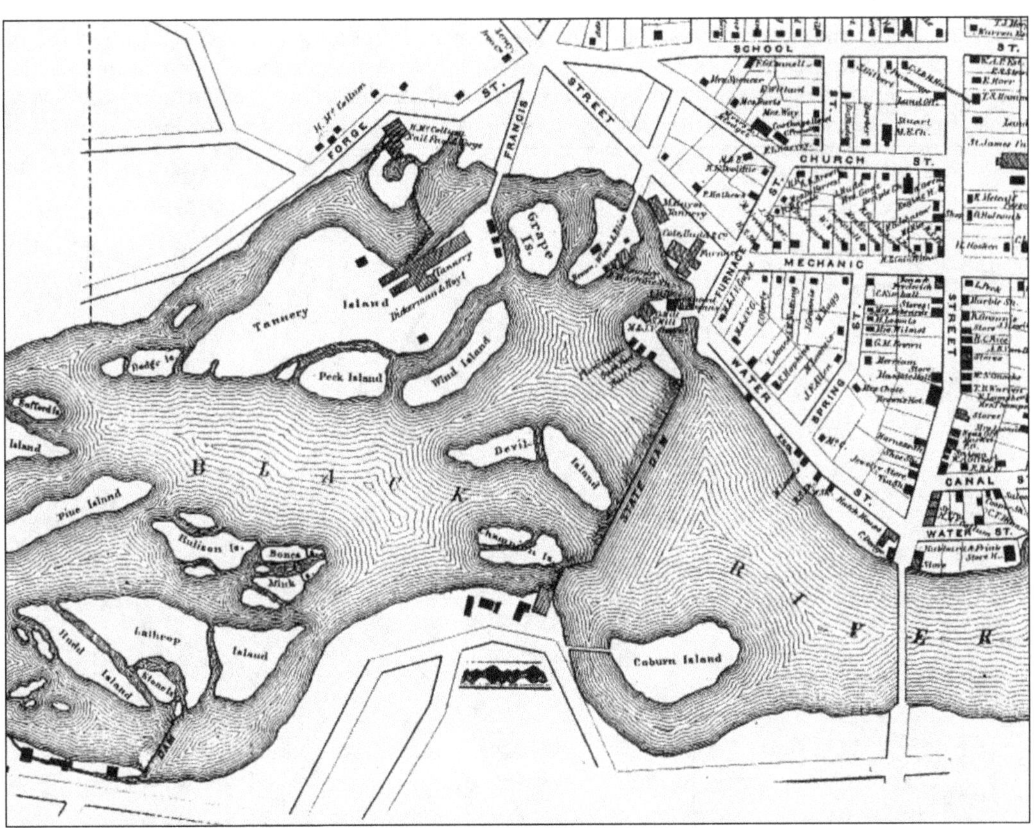

There are 29 islands scattered among the rapids of the Long Falls. The river did more than furnish power for industry; it also brought raw materials needed for the mills and carried the products that were made to markets. Log booms, strung across the river above the falls, had millions of feet of logs behind them waiting to be fed into the mills. The islands themselves are as varied as their names; some huddle together in midstream, some hug the banks, and some are isolated and abandoned.

ELECTRIC LIGHT STATION. GUYOT'S PLANING MILL. CARTHAGE WATER WORKS PUMPING STATION.

Guyot Island was named for Bazille Guyot, a native of Troyes, France, who arrived in 1816; this island is located close to the east shore just below the State Dam. In 1816, Guyot and Louis Bryant built a forge, the first industry on any of the islands. They also erected a sawmill for James LeRay, and in 1833, they erected a gristmill. At Guyot's death, his sons Victor and Frederick took over the island. Through the years, the island has furnished sites for a nail works (begun in 1828), forge, rolling mill, gristmill, ax factory, carding mill, broom handle factory, furniture factory, custom and repair shops for machinery, and turning mill. Guyot Island and Furnace Island were the first places to catch fire on the east side of the river during the great fire of 1884.

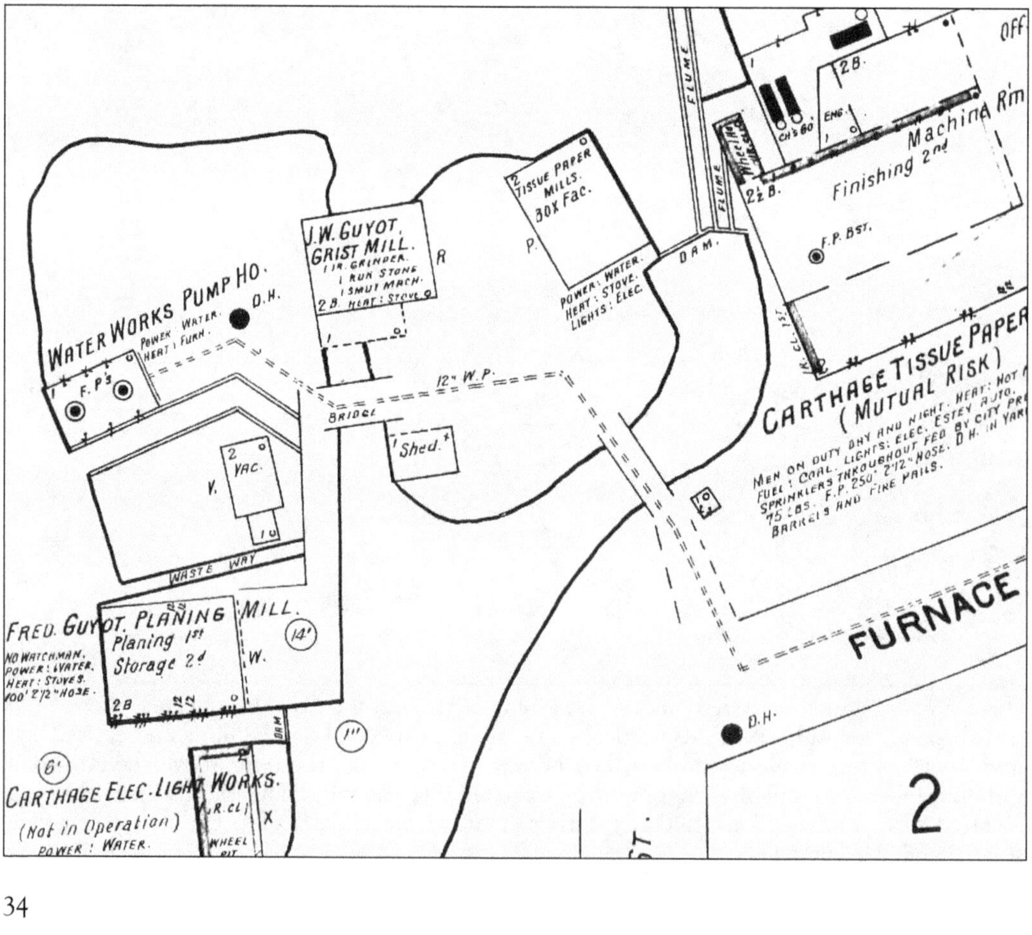

Tannery Island was the second island to be utilized as an industrial site. In 1830, Walter Nimrocks and Allen Peck built a tannery on the island, giving it its name. The largest of the islands, it is located along the eastern shore near the old Carthage Machine Company. About 1832, James P. Hodgkins and Calvin Auburn erected a foundry just below the tannery, drawing water from the same flume. Samuel J. Davis also erected a small iron shop on the island. Hodgkins and Auburn sold out to Joseph Crowner in 1834, who began the manufacture of plows. About 1874, a mineral spring was discovered on Tannery Island, at a depth of 275 feet. In 1896, Peter Yousey, Peter McQuillen, and Augustus Maxwell formed the Island Paper Mill. This reflected the move from ironworks and tanneries to pulp and paper.

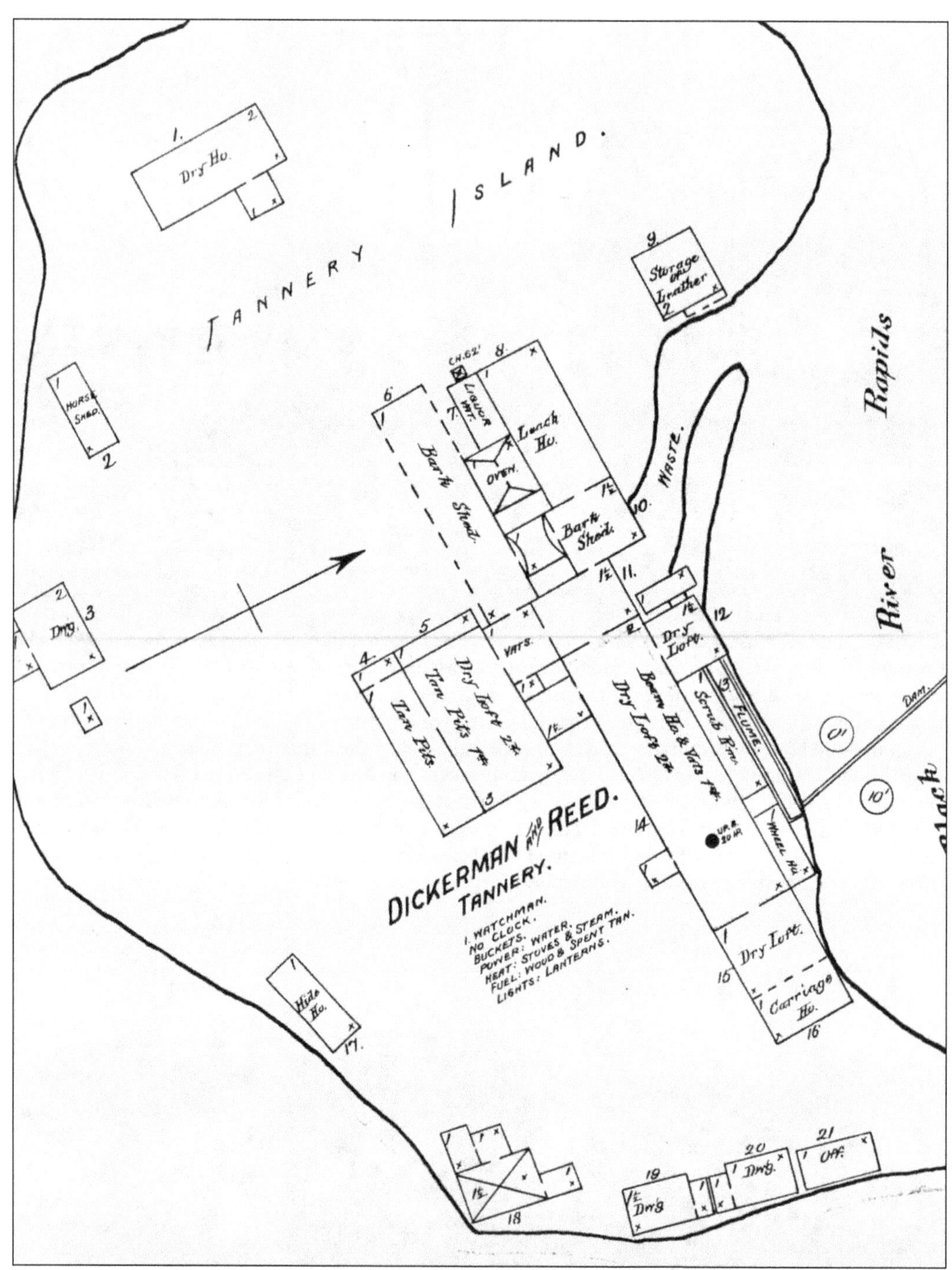

This map intended for firemen shows the placement of buildings on Tannery Island in 1890. The actual maps were in color, letting people know the type of construction and any hazardous materials that might be stored there. Other information contained is whether there is a watchman, the type of power and fuel, and the manner of lighting. The presence of water buckets is also indicated. The Dickerman Tannery was the largest and last of the tanneries on this island and was eventually lost in a spring flood.

IRON WORKS OF RYTHER & PRINGLE.

In 1845, James P. Hodgkins gave Furnace Island its name by erecting a foundry for the purpose of producing the huge castings necessary for Hiram McCollum's new rolling mill and nail works. In 1852, Ezra Hodgkins and Levi Wood installed a lathe and planer, inaugurating the era of the machine shop. George Ryther and James Pringle owned it at the time of the great fire of 1884 and reacted to the destruction by erecting a bigger and better machine shop on the same spot. This shop was finally destroyed by fire in 1953. The map below shows Ryther and Pringle Company in 1902.

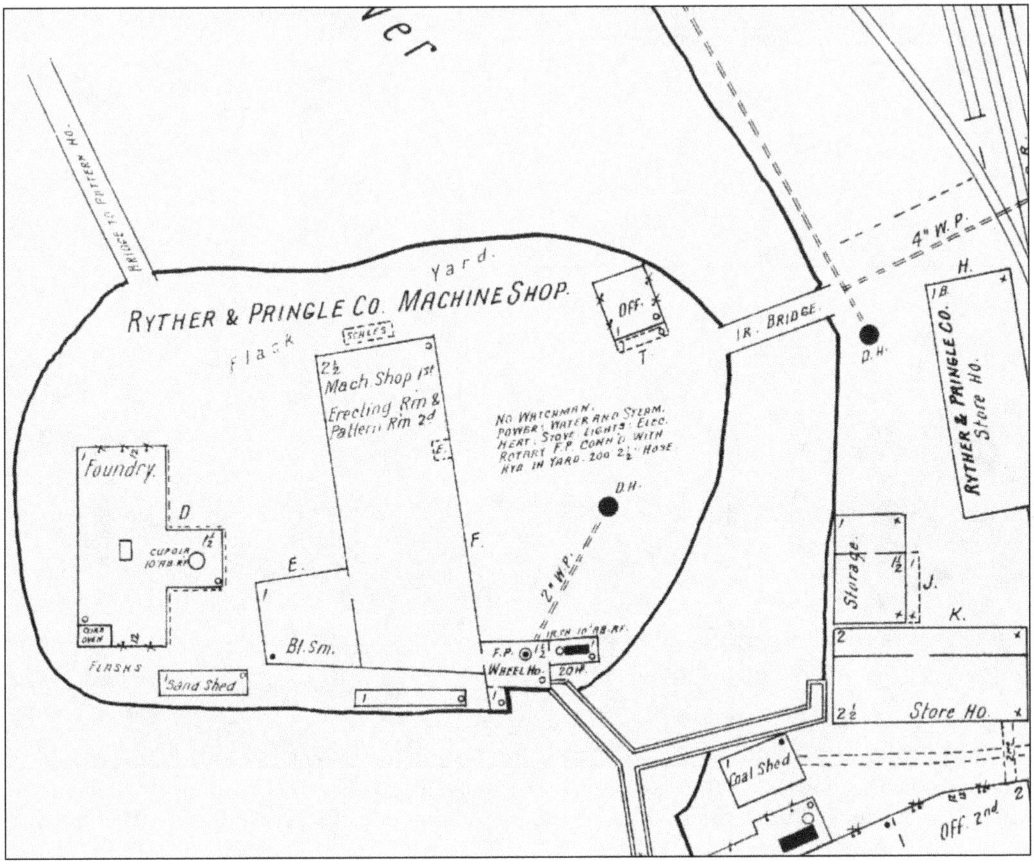

Coburn is the only island located above the State Dam. Never used as a mill site, William Coburn and a Mr. Rulison had a lumberyard on it connected with their sawmill. The sawmill was built in 1852 on the shore below the home William Coburn built in 1860. Technically, Coburn Island is no longer an island, as the channel has been filled in and is now part of the railroad yard for Carthage Papermakers.

Wood was floated downriver from as far as Port Leyden and as near as Castorland to Carthage, where it was removed from the river to be used as lumber or pulp, depending on the type and quality. (Meyer collection.)

Above is an example of early factories taking advantage of the hydropower of the Black River. Below is a picture of a boat being lowered into the Black River from the railroad bridge. Taken about 1900, it was an event that needed many men and attracted as many spectators. This boat was designed for the St. Regis Rossing Plant, located in the area of the current West Carthage boat launch. (Town of Champion Archives.)

Near the eastern shore between Furnace and Tannery Islands is tiny Grape Island. A small storehouse was on this island as late as the 1960s. Other islands (none of which ever supported industry) are Peck, Dodge, Lathrup, Budd, Bones, Rulison, Devil, Wind, Champion, Stone, and Mink Islands. Some were named for prominent families, while others may have been given names by early surveyors prior to 1864 when they appeared on a survey map. The map below is from *Stone's Atlas of 1864*.

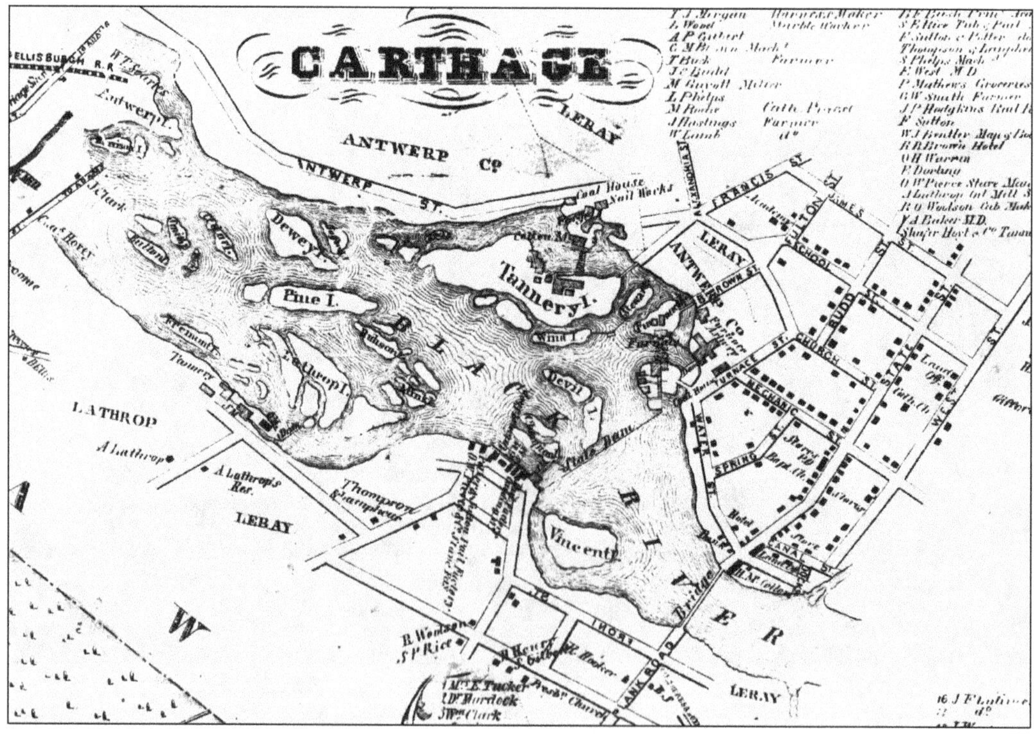

This early picture of the State Bridge and the railroad bridge (left foreground) has Coburn Hill identified as the background. The wing on that building places this before 1930. On the south side of Bridge Street, the Farrar House (presently the Scherer Funeral Home) and the Marcus Mason Mansion (present site of the Carthage Area Hospital Outreach and VA Clinic) are seen. (Michael Perfetto Jr. collection.)

Taken from the west side, this *c.* 1940 picture shows the Carthage waterfront with the spires of several churches and the fire hall dominating the horizon. (Bob Blunden collection.)

Eventually the ferry of Jean Baptiste Bossuot was replaced with a number of bridges, beginning with the first one, a toll bridge built by Ezra Church in 1812–1813 for the Turnpike Company. When the bridge was completed, the privilege of the first crossing was let and the highest bidder was Elijah Fulton of West Carthage, who gave a gallon of rum for the privilege of driving the first team across the bridge. "There was high times while the rum lasted," according to an article in the *Carthage Republican*. In 1828, Vincent LeRay and Joseph Budd led a group of local businessmen who erected a series of bridges from island to island. In this picture of the McCollum Block (below left) and ladies shopping, the entrance to the State Bridge can be seen; this is the bridge that replaced the hoop bridge in 1896.

Four

Paper and Related Industries

James A. Outterson was a significant figure in the North Country paper industry. Between 1897 and 1904, he constructed and managed four paper mills and one sulphite pulp mill in the twin villages. All told, he was responsible for forming or operating 15 pulp or paper mills in Jefferson and Lewis Counties. Above is a sketch of the tissue mill done in 1907. (Metro Paper Industries collection.)

In 1911, James A. Outterson merged the Carthage Sulphite and Pulp Company and the LeRay Paper Company (located on adjacent lots in West Carthage) into the Carthage Sulphite Pulp and Paper Company. The map below shows the location.

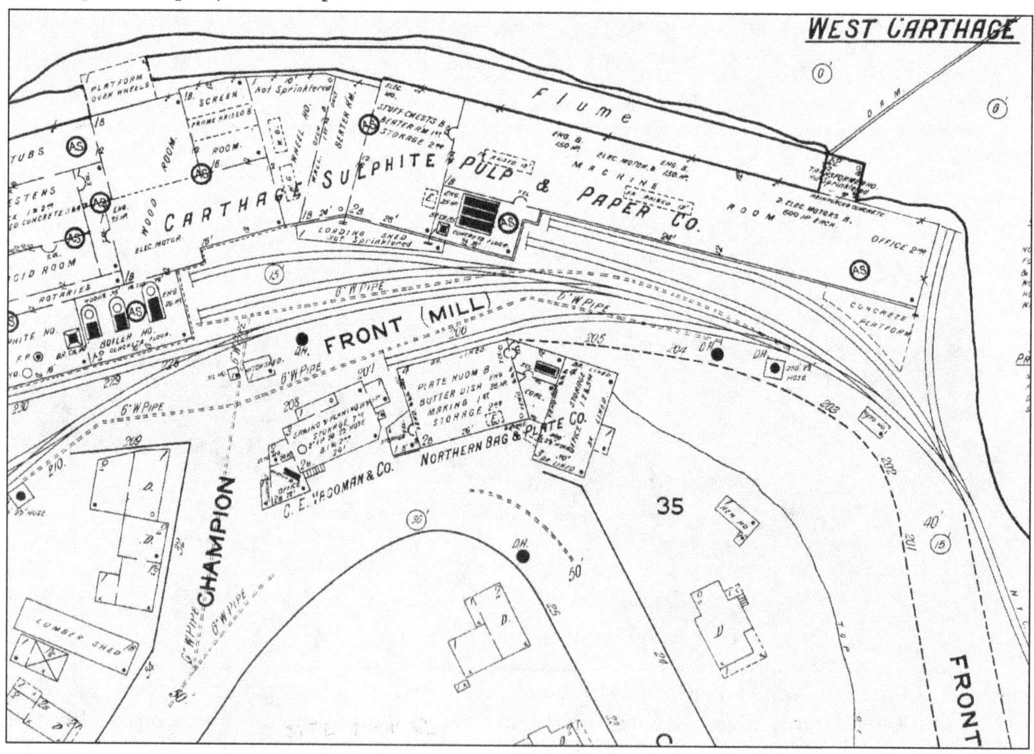

An interior shot of the machine room of the LeRay paper mill, taken about 1900, shows the inside of the building below. The multiple windows allowed for natural light on the massive papermaking machines. (Town of Champion Archives.)

The brick and steel plant was greatly expanded after Outterson acquired it. It is an example of "slow-burning construction," a method of fireproof building that placed the mill firmly in the 20th century in terms of design and the direct opposite of the multistory wooden mill structures of mid-century.

Urban C. Hirschey helped establish Climax Manufacturing Company, begun by his brother Samuel. Urban became president of the company upon his brother's death in 1918. The company took advantage of the explosion in packaging to expand its operation and acquired an idle mill in West Carthage, now Carthage Papermakers. (Bob Blunden collection.)

In 1902, James A. Outterson established the West End Paper Company. The firm constructed a mill on the site of Dr. F. E. Robinson's pulp casket plant and equipped it with the latest papermaking machine. Robinson's house can be seen in the left background. (Town of Wilna Archives.)

In 1914, the Zellerbach family of California obtained the rights to a newly developed towel machine and needed to expand. In 1915, 23-year-old James David Zellerbach came to Carthage where he leased space in a brick building on Water Street and, with one machine, began the National Paper Products Company.

By 1917, with a railroad siding constructed and additional converting machines, the plant had 35 employees and was producing 3,000 cases of toweling weekly. This was the birthplace of the National Paper Products Company's operations. When that company went bankrupt in 1917, Zellerbach bought it to protect its eastern supply of paper. This picture shows a 0-60-type shifter engine. (Town of Champion Archives.)

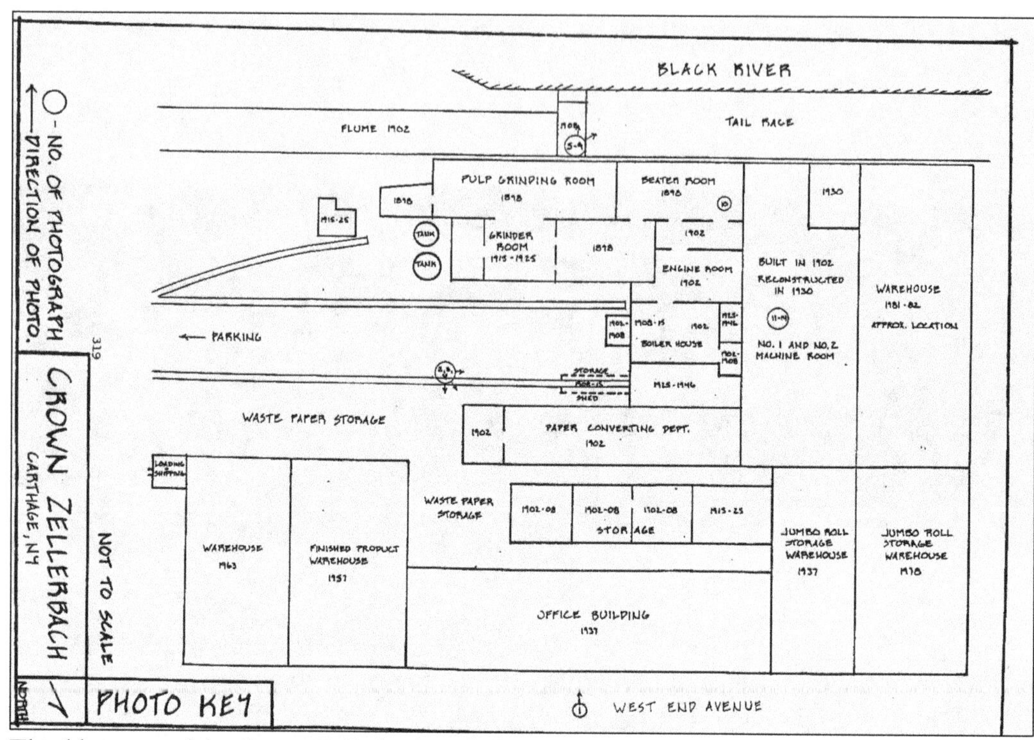

This blueprint of the Crown Zellerbach mill shows when each section was built, beginning with the 1897 constructions of Dr. F. E. Robinson, the 1902 additions of James A. Outterson, and ending with the 1963 warehouse. An exterior sketch from 1900 was made from the river side of the mill. (Metro Paper Industries collection.)

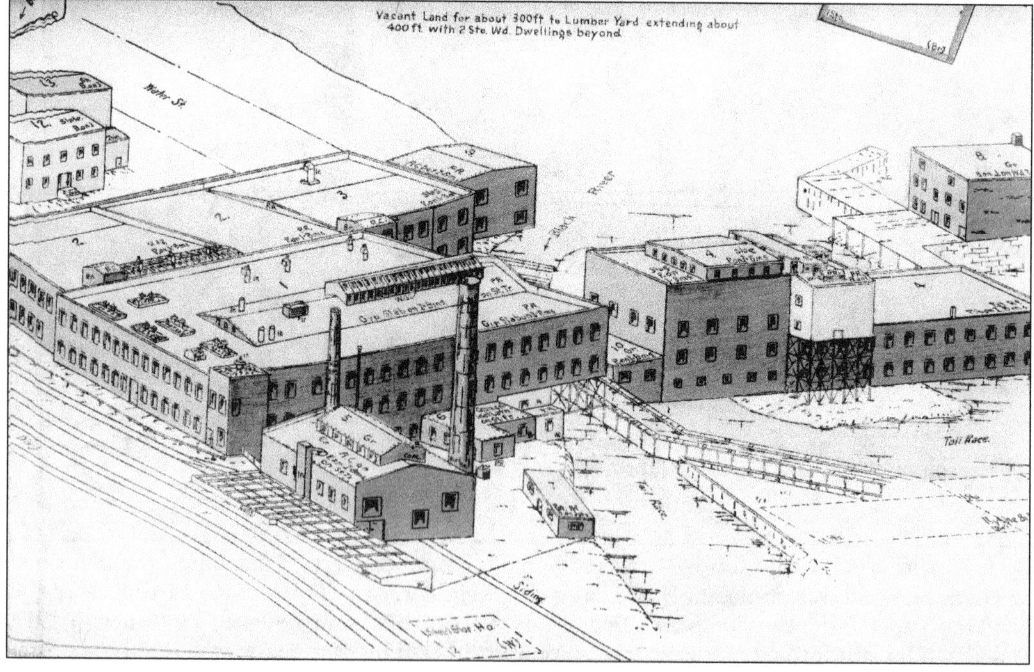

Men of the LeRay Paper Company mill in 1900 are pictured in the yard. The second from the left in the fourth row is Ray Rogers, and to the extreme right of the first row is Will Van Brocklin. The picture on the bottom shows logs stockpiled in the yard of the sulphite mill. In 1899, this mill employed 60 men, consumed 15,000 cords of wood per year, and had a gross output of 27 tons per day or about 17 million pounds of pulp per year.

In January 1897, Wooster O. Ball, W. Drullard Ball, and a half-brother, Arthur Rae Ball, joined James A. Outterson in organizing the Carthage Tissue Paper Mills Company and acquired the sawmill of Augustus Kesler, turning that facility into a paper mill. By 1899, they were producing 15 tons of tissue paper ever 24 hours. Charles Pratt was chief executive officer in 1934 when the mill closed. The picture below, taken at the sulphite mill about 1900, shows the tremendous piles of logs needed to produce paper.

This aerial view of the Black River and the State Dam shows the tendency of mills to acquire their own woodland supply. This led to overcutting in many areas. Spruce was especially prized and was more difficult to find as much had been harvested for the lumbering industry. In fact, it was once said that "there is a paper mill now where once there was a saw mill." Many of the mills acquired land in the Adirondack Mountains, and some still maintain those interests today. Sending the logs downriver to the mills provided work for many, and there are some timber-related industries in the area, but the days of harvesting trees for paper are gone. (Heritage Room Collection.)

At the rossing plant, the pitch from the spruce was removed to prevent it from gumming up the paper machinery. (Town of Champion Archives.)

The North Country has also spawned paper machine manufacturing plants. The Carthage Machine Company (initially known as the Wendler Machine Company) was established in 1892 and from its inception made wood chippers, debarkers, and grinding machines for paper mills locally and, in later years, worldwide.

Built in 1894, the original two-story brick structure of the Wendler Machine Company typifies the paper mill buildings constructed in the 1890s in northern New York State. In 1899, James A. Outterson purchased the mill and changed its name to Carthage Machine Company.

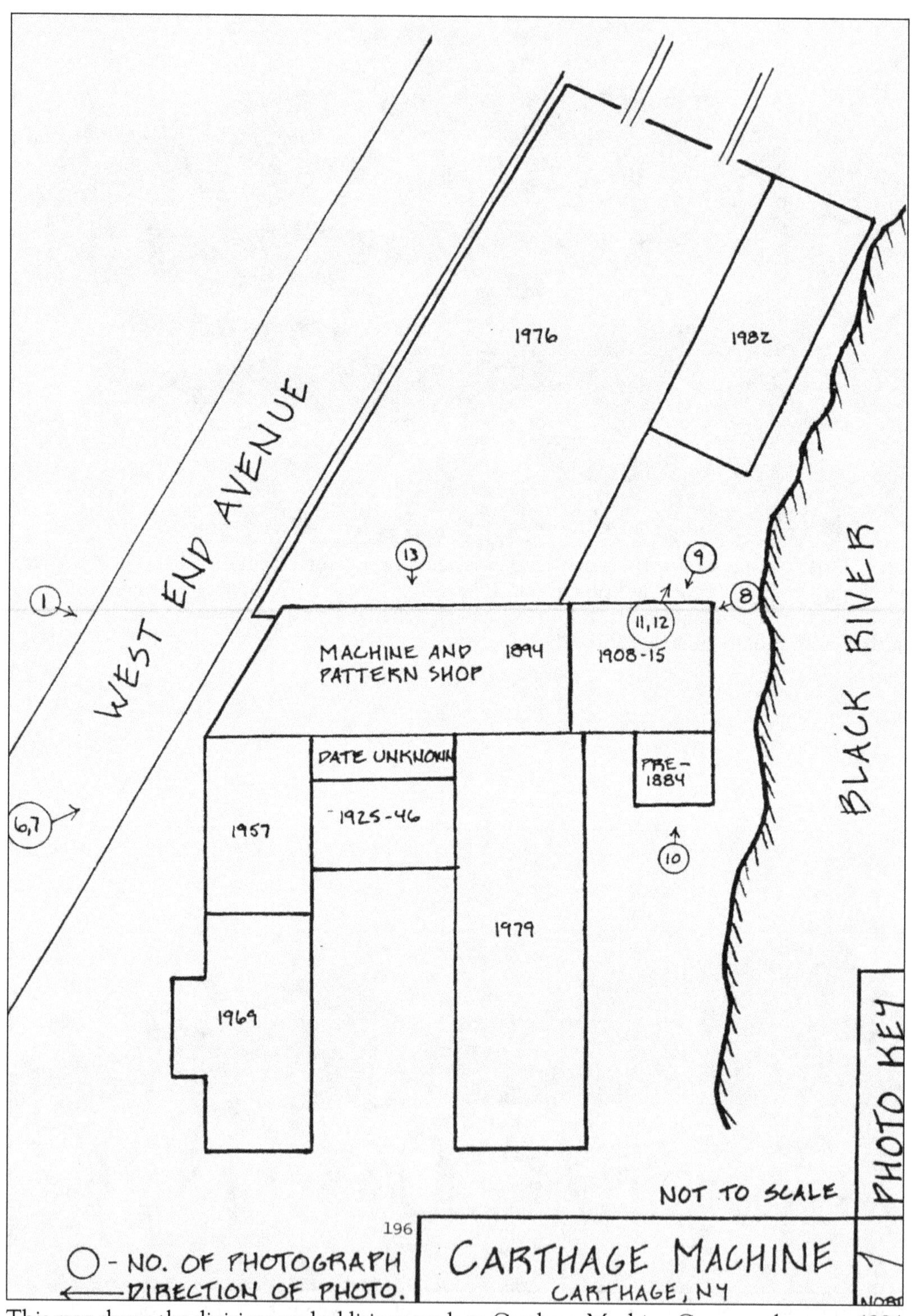

This map shows the divisions and additions made to Carthage Machine Company between 1884 and 1982. The business is still in operation on West End Avenue as CEM.

Shown is one of the dams on the Black River that provided power for the mills. The railroads opened up a much wider market for the products made by the various mills. (Town of Champion Archives.)

Climax Manufacturing on Champion Street in West Carthage is seen here in a 1970s picture. The following pictures depicting the papermaking process are also from its archives and, although undated, are from the 1960s and 1970s. (Climax Manufacturing archives.)

In some respects, papermaking remained the same throughout the 20th century. The picture above shows paper machines around 1900 at the LeRay mill. The one below was taken about 1950. (Below, Climax Manufacturing archives.)

In the beater room, recycled paper is made into paper stock. This machine turns it into a pulp. (Climax Manufacturing archives.)

This machine pumps stock (pulp) from one section of the mill to another. (Climax Manufacturing archives.)

This is part of the wet end, where stock is made into paper. Suction boxes above remove water by vacuum. (Climax Manufacturing archives.)

In the dryer section, paper comes onto forming board and then goes through superheated dryers to the finish end of the machine. (Climax Manufacturing archives.)

Shown here is the wet end, before the dryers. (Climax Manufacturing archives.)

Here is where the wet end meets the dry end. The paper on the left is still wet. The dark vertical section is the felt and begins the drying process. (Climax Manufacturing archives.)

Workers check tension on a roll. (Climax Manufacturing archives.)

Granite rolls flatten paper and make it uniform thickness. (Climax Manufacturing archives.)

This is the dry end of paper machine; seen is the finish end with rolls visible. (Climax Manufacturing archives.)

The slitter is cutting and rewinding from a roll. (Climax Manufacturing archives.)

This is machine room No. 5 of the National Paper Products West End Division, looking southwest at the wet end, taken in 1930. (Town of Wilna Archives.)

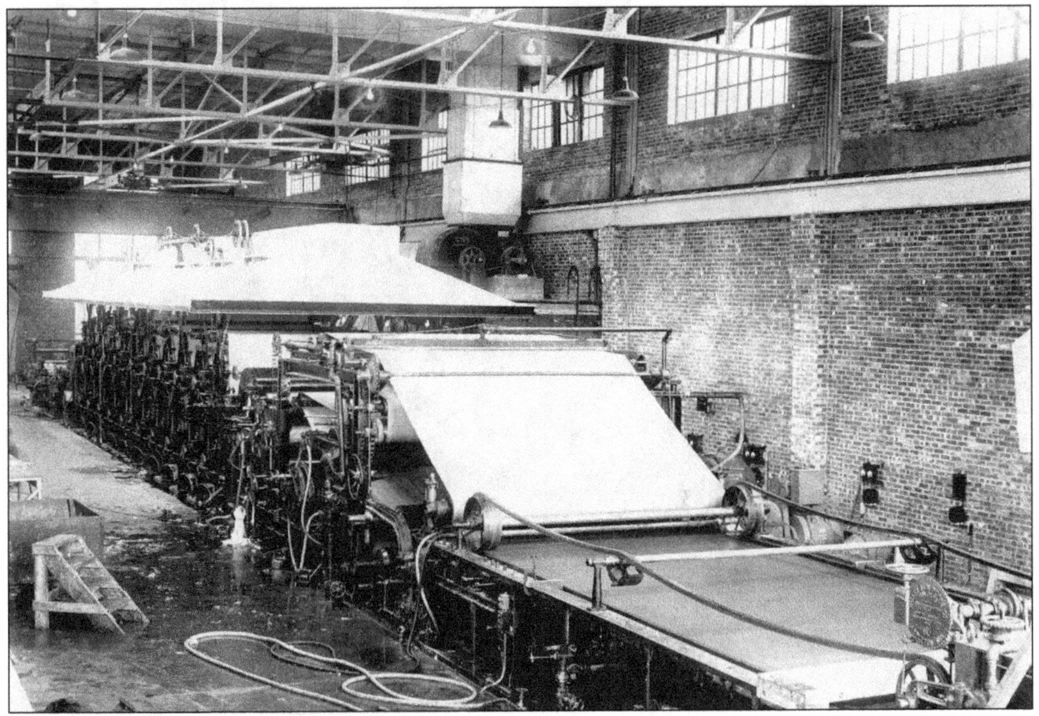

Seen here is National Paper Products West End Division, machine room No. 5, taken in February 1930. (Town of Wilna Archives.)

This is the National Paper Products West End Division power substation, taken in May 1930. (Town of Wilna Archives.)

Seen here is National Paper Products West End Division machine No. 5, the drive aisle. This image was taken in April 1940. (Town of Wilna Archives.)

Five

Industrial Parade of 1912

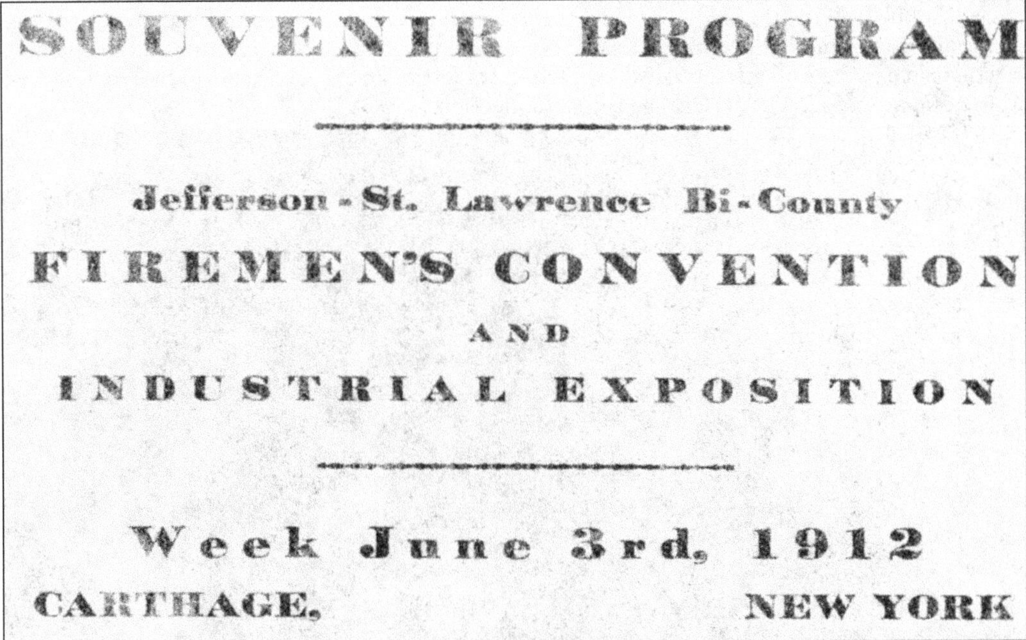

SOUVENIR PROGRAM

Jefferson - St. Lawrence Bi - County

FIREMEN'S CONVENTION

AND

INDUSTRIAL EXPOSITION

Week June 3rd, 1912

CARTHAGE, NEW YORK

The year 1912 saw the largest parade ever held in Carthage. A combination of the firemen's convention and industrial exposition, it was a weeklong event with different scheduled activities and a themed parade each day. The local newspapers listed every float, including its decorations and occupants, every car that appeared in Saturday's automobile parade, and a play-by-play of the featured ball game between the Carthage Red Arrow team and the New York Airbrake team of Watertown. (Heritage Room Collection.)

The reviewing stand for the automobile parade was set up in front of the light and power building in the middle of the south side of State Street. At 4:00 p.m., the automobile parade formed on Mechanic Street, passing to West Street as far as Thorpe Street, turning into State Street, through State and Bridge Streets, then through West Carthage and back to Carthage, eventually returning to Mechanic Street. It is estimated that 4,000 people witnessed the parade, in which 45 cars were all attractively decorated. It was estimated that the cars in line represented an investment of $125,000. (Heritage Room Collection.)

President of the village Charles W. Strickland headed the parade of cars. In the image below, Eugene McDonald, father of Rita McLean of Bridge Street, drives a Hudson filled with children. Rose McDonald is in the middle back. The car is passing the Dunlap building, the present Cigar Store next to St. James' Roman Catholic Church. (Rita McLean collection.)

Among the cars were Franklin roadsters, Oakland touring cars, and Overland vehicles. Fred Lanphear drove a Babcock touring car owned by John McDonald. Dr. G. D. Hewitt drove a Ford; other local men in the parade were Seth M. Strickland, I. Mendelssohn, Thomas Coyle, Fred Goutremont, William Squires, and E. C. Crooks. Below, police are present, but newspapers reported no crime during the weeklong celebrations. (Heritage Room Collection.)

The 500 children of the Carthage school followed the F. R. Schmidt's band of Watertown for the children's parade, Thursday at 3:00 p.m. Behind the band were three youths with a banner reading Carthage High School. Then marched small children of the school in two long parallel lines holding a rope of orange and black (the school colors) to keep straight lines. (Heritage Room Collection.)

Scattered along the marching line were older boys carrying banners reading History, English, Geography, and Arithmetic. The sign carriers were all costumed. (Heritage Room Collection.)

The Carthage High School athletes were next in line, with the football team being followed by the baseball team, and at various intervals, the school yells were given by the boys under the direction of chief leader H. F. O'Keefe. A huge American flag carried by one of the boys followed the training class, and the domestic science class was next; a huge lettered sign supported at each end by brooms preceded them. (Heritage Room Collection.)

The Dramatic Club was next in line, and all the members were in costume. Helen Carter, dressed as Mother Goose, rode at the head of the club on a Shetland pony. Geraldine Outterson and Helen Balmat were Native American maiden outriders; the rest of the club members marched on foot and were clad to represent nearly all nationalities. (Heritage Room Collection.)

The high school training class, dressed in pure white with purple and orange sashes, came next. Behind it was the domestic science class also wearing white and sporting little white caps. At the end of this section, in a horse-drawn carriage, were Esther Parker as a cook and Persia DeCant as a housewife. (Heritage Room Collection.)

The industrial parade was held on Thursday at 4:00 p.m. Four horses drew the Carthage Sulphite Pulp and Paper Company's float. Two attendants, dressed in blue pants and white coats, walked at the heads of the first team. The float showed roll paper, pulpwood, and tag board, and small oyster pails were strung around the top of it. (Heritage Room Collection.)

D. J. Renaud and Son showed a fine casting on a well-decorated wagon. Renaud's foundry and machine shop specialized in brass and iron castings and lead and aluminum jigs (both made and recut); boiler grate bars were also a specialty. It advertised "work done while you wait." It was followed by the Ryther and Pringle float, displaying a shredder, and Carthage Machine Company's float containing a chipper. (Heritage Room Collection.)

The Jefferson Chair Company had a very attractive display of chairs. It was followed by Wilna Furniture Company's float showing buffets. Next came the Northern Bag and Plate Company's float with machines making pulp pie plates and paper butter dishes. (Heritage Room Collection.)

An automobile trimmed up with bunting and filled with lady employees represented John Noland's Boston Store. D. G. Wilson, a druggist, had a fine float, with two of his clerks on it, mixing colored waters. (Heritage Room Collection.)

Schlieder Florist's beautiful float is shown passing the Grand Union Hotel on the right. People observe the parade from the balcony, as well as on the porch and street level. (Heritage Room Collection.)

The Champion Paper Company's float was painted white, even the drapery for the horses and the driver's suit being white. Large rolls of paper stood on the wagon. Behind it, the West End Paper Company's float had a roll of paper containing four miles of paper, enough for 10,909 copies of the *Carthage Republican*. (Heritage Room Collection.)

Behind the masks (or under them) of the Sherwin Williams Colormen were local lads. From left to right are unidentified, Stanley Phalen, Leslie Virkler, and DeWitt Coburn. The man with the horse is unidentified. (Michael Perfetto Jr. collection.)

At the end of the parade was a rig drawn by a team of oxen in which the village's two oldest inhabitants, Pierre G. Depeyster and Orville Cutler, were riding. The message on the wagon said, "We saw Carthage 100 years ago." (Heritage Room Collection.)

Each evening's celebration ended with the "grand illumination" and a band concert. The illuminations were a great feature of the occasion, and few villages in the state could equal them, because of the expense. Everyone especially admired State Street. (Heritage Room Collection.)

On the last night, at the conclusion of the fireworks, all the lights in the vicinity of Mechanic and State Streets were turned out, and a bell began to toll. Gradually a set of colored lights on an elk's head and a B.P.O.E. sign were lit, and as the lights attained full candlepower, Schmidt's band played "Auld Lang Syne." (Heritage Room Collection.)

Six

Churches of the Twin Villages

An interior photograph of St. James' Roman Catholic Church is seen here, taken before the addition of the marble altar and railings that were made possible through the bequest of Jenny Carroll Galvin. She left money for three marble altars, a pulpit, and a communion rail in the will that went to probate in June 1947.

The present St. James' Roman Catholic Church was begun in 1864 on the same site as the previous church, which had been purchased by the Episcopal Society and moved by it. Rev. Michael Barry had charge of the construction of the church, which was accomplished through the efforts of village men under the leadership of Arnold Galleciez.

The St. James' Parochial School opened in 1886, with an enrollment of about 50 pupils under the supervision of the Sisters of St. Joseph, with Reverend Mother Josephine in charge. The convent is shown to the right of the school.

The first Baptist Church of Carthage was originally an offshoot of the Baptist Society of Champion Village and was formed on February 9, 1839. It was located on several sites before locating at the present spot. After burning in 1884, the current church was built the following year but was extensively improved in 1921, due in part to an endowment by Deacon F. A. Southwick.

Shown is the Methodist Episcopal church. The original building on this site was a large frame building erected in 1873 at a cost of $50,000. It was dedicated on November 11, 1873 (below), but proved to be of weak construction and was replaced by the present building in 1893. The roof caught fire in 1884, but the pastor and parishioners managed to save it.

Originally the Grace Episcopal congregation purchased and moved the first St. James' Roman Catholic Church across State Street in 1866 and used it until it burned in 1884. Work on the present church was begun immediately, and in 1888, the rectory was built next door. In 1915, excavation was done for the large basement, or undercroft, housing the parish hall. (Jeannie Fox collection.)

Grace Episcopal Church without its spire is seen here. After the fire of 1884, the pastor asked the public to bring him any bits of the melted bell, intending to reuse them in recasting the bell. A legend had arisen around these artifacts that each drop from the bell had fallen into the shape of the cross. It is not recorded whether old metal was used in the new bell.

Originally the First Congregational Church was organized by Rev. Nathaniel Dutton in 1835 with 12 members. It was built in 1852 and enlarged in 1893 by the Congregational Society. Over the years, the Universalist and the United Christian congregations have used it. The present chancel was added in 1956. It was organized as Long Falls Baptist Church in 1982.

The First Presbyterian Church began as the First Congregational Society in March 1835. A division of the membership took place in 1851 and the Presbyterians purchased an old blue barn from Patrick S. Stewart on North School Street and converted it into a church. In 1852, the Congregationalists regrouped and built the church shown on the previous page. The Presbyterian church was destroyed in the fire of 1884, and the present church was built on the corner of Church and School Streets the following year. In 1923, the Congregationalists merged with the Universalists, and a second merger occurred in 1968 reuniting the Congregationalists and Presbyterians. (*The Growth of a Century*.)

OLD TIME REVIVAL
AND
GOSPEL OF HEALING

SIGNS WONDERS ! MIRACLES !

"Come with your burdens.... Carry away a smile"

"Bring the sick for prayer.... Jesus heals"

R. C. Stutenroth
Musical Director

Bertha D. Brown
Pianist

EVANGELIST R M. SHEARER

A REVIVAL OF OLD TIME RELIGION

"Jesus Christ the same yesterday--TODAY and forever"

INTER-DENOMINATIONAL——EVERYBODY INVITED——ALL SEATS FREE

OPERA HOUSE, MECHANIC ST., CARTHAGE, N. Y.

Beginning Sunday Afternoon at 2:30, March 23–Every Night in the Week at 7:30

Calvary Assembly of God began with interdenominational revivals held in the opera house under the guidance of evangelist R. M. Shearer. At first, the meetings were held in a temporary building called the tabernacle; in 1937, a more permanent building was called the Calvary Tabernacle. In 1946, the congregation moved to Christ Church of 8 Madison Street, and in 1962, it built what ultimately became its school on Martin Street Road. The current church was dedicated in November 1980. (Calvary Assembly of God.)

Seven

Fires and Fire Departments

About 11:10 a.m. on October 20, 1884, the first alarm was sounded from West Carthage when fire was discovered at the sash and blind factory. Volunteer firemen responded quickly with a steamer and two hose carts, but the fire was spreading fast and had already reached Farrar's tub factory and the Meyer and Ross furniture factory. (Edith Meyer collection.)

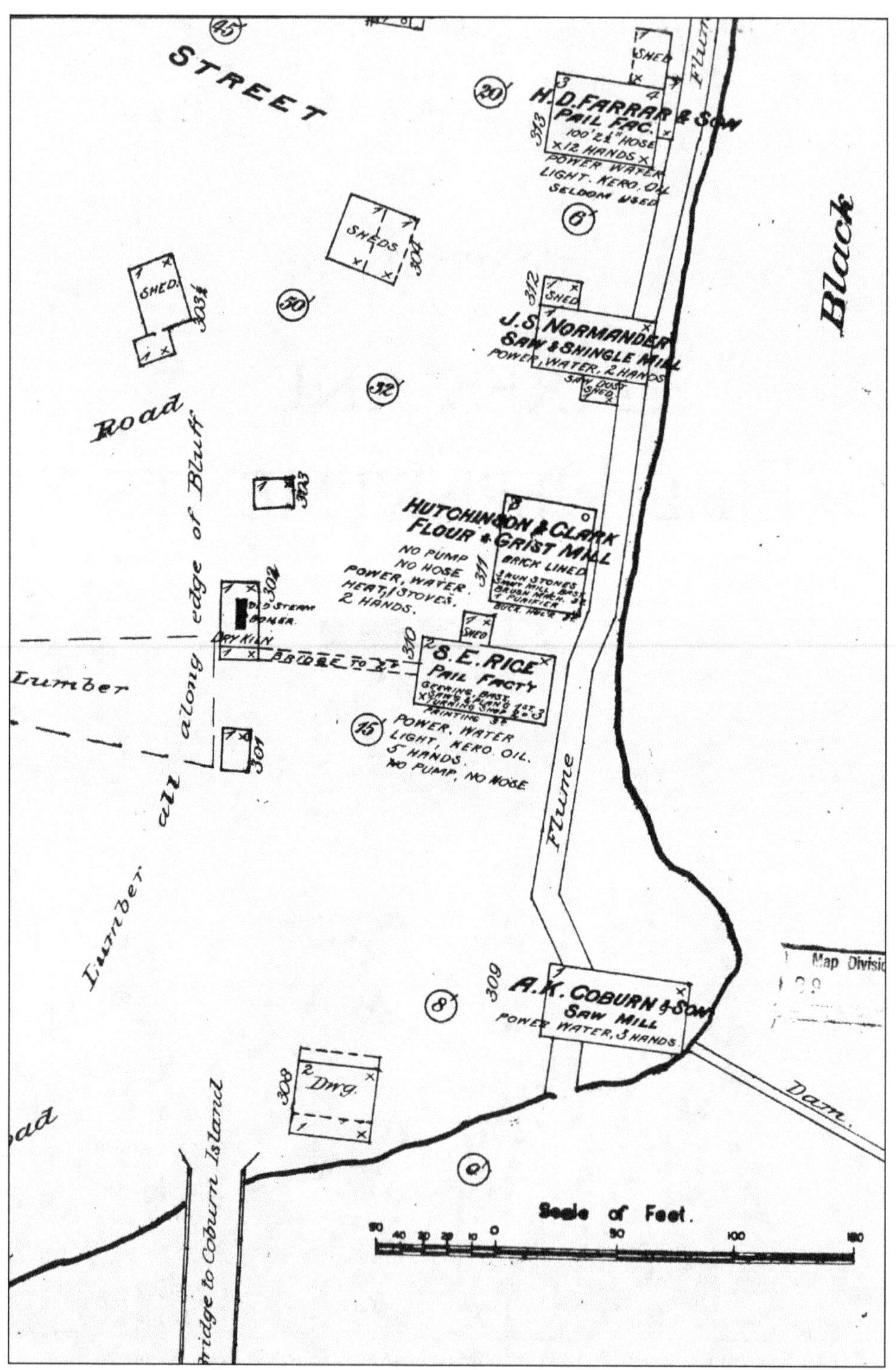

This map shows the mills from the State Dam to about Lathrop Street in West Carthage in July, three months before the 1884 fire. It shows the proximity of the mills and their closeness to the river. Not shown are the islands. The map on page 33 gives the proper perspective.

By now, the Carthage firemen who had answered the West Carthage alarms were hurrying back across the bridge to begin fighting the fire that had come ashore. Word was telegraphed to Watertown, Lowville, Boonville, and Utica; help was needed in Carthage. The railroad tracks were cleared of other traffic so they could be used to bring firemen and equipment to Carthage. Watertown came first with 30 firemen, the No. 2 steamer (shown above), and 1,000 feet of hose. They came by freight car, and the trip took them 25 minutes. Lowville arrived next, also with 30 men, another 1,000 feet of hose, and their new steamer. Next to arrive was Boonville. Chief William Cole of Watertown realized that the firemen of Carthage were very tired and that they had just about run out of water. Using the 1,000 feet of hose he had brought, Chief Cole began pumping water from the Black River. He pumped this up State Street, which was now threatened by the fire that had moved quickly up from the riverbank. (Town of Wilna Archives.)

The steamer from Lowville began pumping water from the pond at Ryther and Pringle on Furnace Island, where the foundry had already burned. The fire burned most of the afternoon, destroying everything from the riverbank to Monument Park and State Street. Sidewalks were wooden and took the fire right to the front doors of homes, which were then burned. Although there were a number of injuries, no one was killed. (CRT archives.)

By late afternoon, firemen were beginning to win. No new fires were breaking out. Chief William Cole let his men return home early in the evening; Carthage firemen remained on duty all night. More than 100 families had lost their homes. Over 70 acres had been burned; 200 buildings, many of them businesses, were lost. People were facing winter without necessities and no way to earn money to replace these things. (Town of Wilna Archives.)

Above is a sketch by an unknown artist. It was drawn from the west bank, at a point between the State Bridge and the New York Central Railroad bridge. (Town of Wilna Archives.)

With one sawmill left, the Coburn Sawmill, men began immediately to cut lumber brought to Carthage by lumbermen who doubled their efforts to keep the mill supplied. H. Van Amber of Castorland opened a lumberyard on the dock. The fall stayed mild and the men who lost their jobs helped rebuild the mills and factories. A new school was begun the next spring and was ready by September 1886.

Carthage Fire Department.

—o—

William McGraw, *Chief Engineer.*

William Bellan, 1*st Assistant.*

A. A. Collins, 2*d Assistant.*

STEAMER CO., NO. 1.

W. W. Sweet, *Foreman.*

James Walsh, *Assistant Foreman.*

George V. Eggleston, *Secretary and Treasurer.*

TIGER HOSE CO. NO. 1.

J. V. Girardin, *Foreman.*

D. M. Burns, *Assistant Foreman.*

William S. Schwartz, *Secretary.*

A. D. VanAntwerp, *Treasurer.*

Information on the Carthage Fire Department as it appeared in the 1899 village directory is seen at left. Below is a certificate of membership from 1896. (Bill Blunden collection.)

Certificate of Membership.

Carthage, N. Y., April 13 1896

This is to certify that Mr. Harris A. Frink was duly elected a member of Rescue Hose No 2 Co., of Carthage Fire Department, at a regular meeting held at their rooms on Monday April 13 1896, and you will please attend their next meeting to be held at their rooms the first Monday in each month and oblige.

A. W. Connoly Sec'y. C. M. Wichard Foreman.

The picture above is of the Carthage Fire Department and band in 1890. In back are the steamer and the horses used to draw it to a fire. In the image below, a dues notice is seen, threatening to drop any member delinquent in dues. In reality, the department was hurting for members during the late 1890s. Indeed, the need was so great that in 1899 the department waived the fee in an effort to attract more men. (Town of Wilna Archives.)

Notice of Dues.

Carthage, N. Y., ... 189

M.......... ....

Dear Sir:—It has been decided to drop from the rolls all members who are in arrears according to the by-laws.

Your arrearage to......................

amounts to ....$............

Fines..................$............

Total.........$............

Please attend our next regular meeting on.........

..........................189

....

Secretary Tiger Hose Co., No. 1.

Pictured are the 1875 members of the Carthage Fire Department and band. This was the year that the Carthage Board of Trustees passed bylaws for organizing and forming a fire department. On April 27, 1875, two hose companies and an engine company were recognized. H. J. Welch was elected chief engineer; he then selected John Norton as first assistant chief and E. H. Meyers as second assistant chief. The companies were called Steamer Company, Tiger Hose No. 1, and Rescue Hose No. 2. In 1897, Welch, now president of the village, antagonized the fire department by urging the disbanding of the Steamer Company since the village had installed a hydrant system. (Bill Blunden collection.)

This 1933 Seagraves ladder truck fought fires in Carthage for 43 years. It had eight ladders, including a 50-foot Bangor ladder that took four to six men to lift. Many residents remember this truck with its twin, a 1933 tanker. The Seagraves was taken out of service in 1976 but was kept for parades until it was sold to Richard J. Blunden of Norwich. It was later acquired by Bill Blunden, a nephew, and returned to Carthage. It is seen below being inspected after its return. (Bill Blunden collection.)

Two views of the Carthage Fire Hall are shown. This building was constructed in 1892. The new tower and bell tower were erected in 1895 at a cost of $850 to "provide suitable alarm for the village." The new tower was used to dry hoses after a fire. This building served as the home of the department for 78 years. (Town of Wilna Archives.)

The building on the right, the second West Carthage School, became the village hall and fire department in around 1908. It remained the village hall and fire department building until the new municipal building was built in 1999 on High Street, across from P&C Plaza. At that time, the building was razed, and a small park was established. (Town of Champion Archives.)

For and in consideration of the sum of One Hundred and Fifty Dollars ($150.00), the receipt whereof is hereby acknowledged, the Citizens' Band Association, so called, of Carthage, hereby transfers, assigns, and sets over unto

West Carthage Fire Department

all the musical instruments, uniforms, and paraphernalia which they acquired from the Fire Department of the Red Mens' Band, so called, of Carthage, but this conveyance is upon condition that the said instruments, uniforms, and paraphernalia shall not be sold to any person, corporation, co-partnership or Association who will remove said property from the village of Carthage or West Carthage, it being understood that this condition is a part of the consideration for the conveyance and transfer of said property.

Dated at Carthage, N. Y., May 14, 1907.

E. H. Austin
Chief West Carthage F.D.

Trustees of W.C.F.D. Band { E. W. Bushnell, L. Besaw

E. Villars for Citizens Band

17 Suits
16 Caps
2 Tubas
1 Baritone
3 altos
1 Trombone
1 Cornet
1 Bass Drum
1 Snare
Desk
Music
Folios
Wagon

The item at left is a receipt for the uniforms and instruments for the West Carthage Fire Department Band. According to the receipt, the uniforms were originally the property of the "Red Mens' Band" of Carthage and then the Carthage Citizens' Band Association. They were acquired on the condition they not be sold out of the area. On the edge of the paper are listed an inventory of items, including 17 suits, 16 caps, 2 tubas, 1 baritone, 3 altos, 1 trombone, 1 coronet, 1 bass drum, 1 snare drum, a desk, music, folios, and a wagon. (Sanderson collection.)

Firematics have always been an integral part of volunteer fire departments in northern New York State. The activities the men participate in are all outgrowths of the way fires originally were fought. Fire pail brigades, efficiency races (carrying the hose, hooking to a source, and aiming the water stream), ladder races, and the like all allowed the men to practice skills while they had a little fun. Taken in 1937 at Tupper Lake, the photograph above shows, from left to right, Peanut Clark, Ed Zecher, Leon Sanderson, Howard Gruner, Charlie Gilligan, and Ron Guyette. The racing vehicle is a 1929 Packard truck. In the event below, firemen must leap from a slowing truck and run to secure the hose to a hydrant while others run to get in position to knock a target down when the water is turned on. (Bill Blunden collection.)

In March 1932, the Carthage Night Hawks drill team was formed and was very successful. After a dormancy of several years, the team was reborn in 1989. It competed in foot drills only. But in 1994, because of a lack of interest, the Night Hawks disbanded, and their equipment was sold to the New Bremen Fire Department. In 1996, the West Carthage Hornets approached the Night Hawks about combining teams due to the manpower shortage. Carthage firefighters had to run under the name West Carthage Hornets, because they had the motorized vehicles to use in the drills. From 1996 until 2007, the combined West Carthage Hornets team has become one of the most successful teams in northern New York State. The team has won 18 drills and has been Jefferson County champions 8 out of the last 10 years. In 2005, the Hornets won the triple crown of drilling. They won Northern New York Convention Championship, Jefferson County Championship, and Overall Points Championship of Northern New York. They had done this several times in the 1960s. (Bill Blunden collection.)

Eight

LATER BUSINESS DISTRICT

Photographer Pierre Meyer captures the downtown of 1910 with its unpaved streets, milling crowds, and bustling business district. This picture was taken from the middle of State Street, standing near today's Cigar Store and looking toward the Strickland Building on the corner of State and South Mechanic Streets. (Heritage Room Collection.)

Reita Taylor is seen here in the late 1940s at the Atlantic Richfield service station at the corner of Bridge and Broad Streets, site of the present McDonald's. Taylor changed oil and pumped gas, as did many women during and after World War II. This site was also home to Adderley Pontiac in the 1950s and 1960s. (Jim Taylor collection.)

Walsemann's Servicenter, on Bridge Street, continued through various ownerships, until it was modernized in 2005 as a restaurant. It last was Station II in 2007. (Village of West Carthage Archives.)

The Blunden-White Agency is shown in a 1974 picture. This is the current location of Fuller Office Supplies on State Street. (Town of Wilna Archives.)

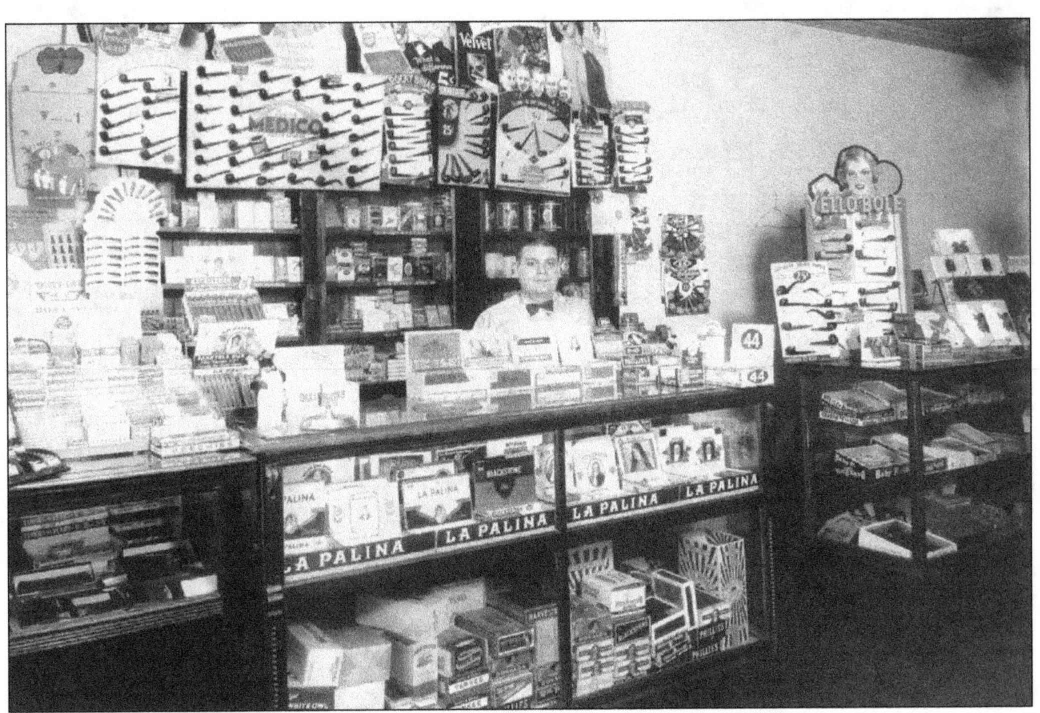

A young Toufee Ellis is shown in his cigar store. People may remember the store in the Grand Union Hotel during the 1950s and 1960s. (Town of Wilna Archives.)

Higman's store on State Street, in this 1939 photograph, later became Gaffney's Ice Cream Parlor. Currently it is the Golden Chang. (Town of Wilna Archives.)

Harriet McManus is seen here in her candy and cigar shop. This was operated out of her home on North Mechanic Street in the 1940s and 1950s. (Town of Wilna Archives.)

What was formerly known as Parker's Laundry was purchased in August 1915 by George Scribner and became the Carthage Laundry. It dealt with commercial, hotel, and family laundry. The main building was located on North School Street near Francis Street. The building was later converted into apartments and eventually was torn down for a parking lot.

The Calender Block is seen here in the early 1920s (above) and during the late 1930s (below). Notice the changes in businesses; W. T. Grant was a prominent fixture for many years, as was California Fruit. (Bob Blunden collection.)

The business known today as the Superior Grill began life around 1900 as a restaurant. In 1915, it is seen here still serving that purpose. Note that the tile floor and the high tin ceiling are in evidence from its earliest days. (Jim Costes collection.)

In 1922, the building was acquired by the John and Mary Costes and became Kandyland, a confectionary shop. John had originally been a salesman traveling in tobacco and coffee; liking the people of Carthage, however, he decided to stay. In the 1930 picture below, a selection of handmade confections offered by the store can be seen. The store was especially noted for its ribbon candy. (Jim Costes collection.)

Nine

People, Places, and Events

West Side Market, run by Ray Bell, second from right, later became Hap Waite's market and the town clerk's office. It is currently the home of the Fabric Cupboard, located at 7 North Main Street in West Carthage. The people seen here are, from left to right, two unidentified women, Mrs. L'Huillier, unidentified, Claire Waite, Ray Bell, and Herbert Bell (Raymond's uncle). (Bell Arnot collection.)

During World War II, Francis Nicholl collected all the steel he could for the war effort. Here is Nicholl standing in front of a pile on South Main Street in West Carthage. In the picture below, George Metzger helps the war effort by cutting wood. This picture was taken on his farm on Avery Road. (Above, CRT archives; below, L. Thornton collection.)

The Carthage Milk and Cream Company was located on the corner of School and Francis Streets. Later this was the location of McKenna's Hardware Store and Harry's Sweet Store; it is across from the freight yard. Below is the Chamberlain Block on School Street. Noah Chamberlain, a well-known contractor, mason, and carpenter, built the imposing multifamily block in the early 1900s. (Town of Wilna Archives.)

Dance recitals have always been a staple of small-town life, but it took the intrepid Vinny King to bring Carthage the minstrel shows of the 1950s. These programs, held at the Strand Theater, featured song and dance by prominent members of the community, including Robert Blunden, George Ablan, Josephine Betrus, Sharlene King, Gerald Dobson, James Dawes, John Scee, Marco Frank, Al Avallone, Mike Michalik, Donald Murphy, Donald Griffith, and many, many more. Below are, clockwise from left, Helen Carron Golden, Arvella Lightholder Gates, Mary Gates, Mary Golden Hynes, and Joan Huff Avalone surrounding maharaja Thomas Maroun in a photograph taken for a Lions Club program in 1950. (Agnes King collection.)

The Strand Theater showed films for over 60 years. The building later became the home of the Branaugh Memorial Boys Club and is currently the Carthage YMCA. Following the war, many people may remember when admission to the movies was a can of food or a bunch of wire coat hangers. (Bob Blunden collection.)

Arthur Post is at his soda fountain located at 252 State Street around 1923. It was named the Hollywood Shop, probably due to its proximity to the Strand Theater (formerly at 250 State). Using business directories, the ownership is shown to change in 1927 to Ralph E. Bennett; in 1930, when it was called Ye Hollywood Shop, M. C. Bennett proprietor; and in 1943, to Harry's Sweet Shop, operated by Harry Liberatos. (Heritage Room Collection.)

Seen here is a transfer party from Maihafer's Bakery to Durkee's Bakery. Pictured are Anne Sayer, Alice Owens, Paul Williams, Hazel Hall, Irene Olds, Sonya ?, Florence Durkee, Al Durkee, Douglas Shampine, Mike Antil, Stuart McFall, Robert Hall, Walt Perkins, Kenneth Schloop, Clinton Schloop, Clifford Gates, Chauncey Lantz, Frank Dennison, ? Montgomery, Shorty Ventrolori, Pete Olds, Bill Longway, and Clesson Pierce. (Sanderson collection.)

Workers from Durkee's Bakery about 1950 are seen here. They are, from left to right, (first row) John Kosztowski, Ray Fairfield, unidentified, Gary Richter, Walter Kosztowski, and Gerald Caldwell; (second row) Ken Rumble, Dave Galvin, Clesson Pierce, unidentified, ? Rumble, Fred Carter, and unidentified; (third row) unidentified, Robert Heinz, Fred Van Patten, George Lanpher, three unidentified men, Stu McFall, unidentified, Paul Williams (president of Durkee's Bakery), and Mike Antil. The unidentified men are drivers from Canton and other places. (Town of Wilna Archives.)

The back of Arnot Hardware Store or Arnot's Plumbing and Heating Company with William Arnot is seen here between 1885 and 1890. This business was succeeded by Bushnell and Bassett. (Delena Schreck collection.)

The Arnot delivery cart, around 1910, is shown traveling up State Street. St. James' Roman Catholic Church is shown in the right rear; the William Perry residence, what later became the Bossuot Funeral Home, is right behind the driver, William Arnot. (Delena Schreck collection.)

The National Hotel, at 214 Church Street, was built about the time of the Civil War and in various forms was a Carthage landmark until the 1884 fire. Known then as the "Stone Jug," it was a stone and wooden structure with a popular bowling alley in the basement. Rebuilt as a three-story building, it was used by Robert Wagner as an emergency hospital during the 1918 influenza epidemic. Most recently, it has been transformed into a medical center for Dr. Jocelyn Aznar-Beane. The 1905 photograph below shows the National Hotel as a three-story building after the renovations. This became the Elks Club in 1949. (Town of Wilna Archives.)

The demolition of the Strickland Building (shown above in 1895) in 1963 occurred 70 years after its construction. In 1931, the Carthage National Bank merged with the National Exchange Bank and Trust Company that was located in the Buckley Building (formerly the National Exchange Bank building) across the street. In 1934, the Market Basket Corporation opened a grocery store (which later became Acme Markets) on the ground floor. The clock on the second floor lived for a time at Paradise Vista, a motel on the way to Fargo. (CRT archives.)

An interior shot of the bar at the Grand Union Hotel is seen here. Frank Pinnizzotto is behind the bar. This was probably taken during the 1950s. (Town of Wilna Archives.)

These unidentified gentlemen are shown at another watering place about 50 years earlier. (Town of Wilna Archives.)

This is a celebratory photograph of some type, taken in front of the opera house on North Mechanic Street. This building was built by the Independent Order of Odd Fellows for its meeting place and was variously used as the opera house, a theater, a youth center, a roller rink, and the home of General Sign Company, until it was finally demolished in 1997. In 1916, the Normander Glove Factory was located on the top floor. Erected in 1906–1907 at a cost of $38,000 and netting $3,500 with its first night performance of *Isle of Bong Bong*, it coincided with the golden age of the paper industry. The photograph at right was taken in 1908. (Heritage Room Collection.)

Dr. Frederick G. Metzger was a Town of Wilna health officer from 1924 to his death in 1940. He is shown above pursuing one of his hobbies; he was the founder of the Carthage Camera Club. Below is a picture of a building quarantined because of small pox. The building may be the back of the opera house, as there is evidence that it was utilized as a hospital in times of epidemics and the window shown is the same type as those seen in the pictures on the previous page. (Metzger collection.)

Joseph P. Brownell, son of C. B., was born in the town of Duanesburg on January 29, 1827. In 1849, he came to Carthage and entered the land office of Vincent LeRay, as an assistant of his uncle Nelson Rulison, who was a surveyor and under whose direction Brownell learned surveying. In 1856, he married Parthenia S., daughter of Osmon Caswell of Theresa, and settled in West Carthage. In 1862, he moved to Croghan in Lewis County, in 1866, he was elected justice of the peace, and in 1870–1871, he served as supervisor of that town. In 1873, he returned to Carthage. In 1876–1877, he served as justice of the peace and then as one of the assessors of the town. He was well known in the county as a surveyor and had been connected with the LeRay land office since 1849. Joseph and Parthenia had three sons, Hiram M., James P., and Charles (Chuckie) M. The young woman in the picture is their daughter May, a teacher at Carthage Academy who died at 31. (Town of Wilna Archives.)

The area called Monument Park was not always a park; it began life as a cemetery (there are still graves of early settlers in the south side of the lot). In November 1890, residents petitioned for a monument to "perpetuate the memory of soldiers and sailors who served in defense of the Union . . . and in the war with Spain." It was not until 1901 that a site was decided upon, and in 1902, the contract for building the monument was awarded to Crooks and McLean. Completed in Barre, Vermont, and shipped by rail to Carthage the following year, it was erected as shown in the photograph, completely by man (and horse) power. The photograph below was taken in 1908 after some landscaping was done. The monument was restored in 2005 through the efforts of local citizens. (Michael Perfetto Jr. collection.)

Ten

Schools and School Groups

This REO bus of the early 1930s was the first school bus in the Carthage school system. It was garaged and serviced by Dominic Condino Motors, after he completed work on his State Street building, which is still run by the family today. (Condino family collection.)

The Augustinian Institute was the forerunner of the Augustinian Academy. This photograph shows the Sisters of St. Joseph convent next to the school. (Heritage Room Collection.)

This is the school built in 1885 to replace the one that burned in the great fire. In the picture above, it is seen in respect to the rest of the village. This school stood on the corner of School and Fulton Streets. Later a high school, seen in the background at right, was built to expand the educational facilities. (Bob Blunden collection.)

The picture above shows a different angle of the Carthage Academy with the addition of the high school building. Below is the "new" elementary school built in 1930. Both the elementary and high school were demolished after the construction of the new Carthage Elementary campus on Beaver Lane to make way for the new Elks Club, built in 1987. (Bob Blunden collection.)

The first West Carthage village school was located on the corner of Champion and Jefferson Streets in 1832 on land donated by A. Champion. The second school (above) was on the corner of Jefferson and Vincent Streets in 1857 and was enlarged 12 years later. The modern building below was built in 1905. In 1929, an addition was made to the school. It contained an auditorium and gymnasium, a home economics department with kitchen, a dining room, and a workshop. (Town of Champion Archives.)

In 1954, a fire destroyed the old part of the West Carthage school. A fire wall separating the new part (built in 1931) from the old stopped the fire from reaching the elementary school. However, the large amount of water used to put out the fire got into the new part, causing a lot of damage. Firemen built makeshift dams of sandbags to steer the water away from the classrooms and into the basement. The inside of the old part was completely destroyed, and only crumbling parts of the walls were left standing. While the fire was at its height, the tin-covered roof collapsed, and the wall facing Jefferson Street tumbled with a roar that sent bricks flying onto the school grounds and street. Fortunately, none of the firemen were injured. Students got the week off. (L. Thornton collection.)

This picture, labeled "Kindergarten School" and taken about 1910, includes Lora Haller, Alice Whaling, Louise Johnson Reeder, Edith Garthe, Helen Phelps Perine, Phil Coyle, Woodin VanAllen, Kathryn O'Keefe, Mable Gleason Fletcher, Katharine Main, Doris Smith, and Dorothea Schmid. The teachers are Edith Porter Russell and Julia Hickox Farmer.

This photograph of the Carthage graduating class of 1911 shows David Balmat, Marion Bocker Valkenburg, Bertha Crowner Ingram, Alma Dickerman Grant, Hazel Parker Post, Adelaide Porter O'Keefe, Leah Sweet Moore, and Muriel Waters Wallace. (Town of Wilna Archives.)

BIBLIOGRAPHY

Allen, Richard S. *Iron Men of Carthage*. Carthage, NY: Carthage Republican Tribune, 1979.

Carthage and West Carthage Directory 1904. Watertown, NY: Kimball Directory Publishing Company, 1904.

Child, Hamilton, comp. *Geographical Gazetteer of Jefferson County, N.Y., 1684–1890*. Syracuse, NY: Syracuse Journal Company, 1890.

Johnson, Julee, and Jeffrey Cody. *Papermaking in the North Country*. Carthage, NY: Village of Carthage, 1986.

Landon, Henry F. *History of the North Country*. Indianapolis: Historical Publishing Company, 1932.

Welsh, William D. *A Brief Historical Sketch of Carthage New York*. Carthage, NY: Carthage Republican Tribune Press, 1941.

West Carthage Centennial 1889–1989. Carthage, NY: Charles H. Weber and Kelsey B. Coffin, 1989.